The
Entrepreneur's Apprentice

Don Darvill

 FriesenPress

Suite 300 - 990 Fort St
Victoria, BC, Canada, V8V 3K2
www.friesenpress.com

Copyright © 2017 by Don Darvill
First Edition — 2016

All rights reserved.

No part of this publication may be reproduced in any form, or by any means, electronic or mechanical, including photocopying, recording, or any information browsing, storage, or retrieval system, without permission in writing from FriesenPress.

Suitcase icon by Gregor Črešnar from the Noun Project

ISBN
978-1-4602-8118-5 (Hardcover)
978-1-4602-8119-2 (Paperback)
978-1-4602-8120-8 (eBook)

1. Business & Economics, Management

Distributed to the trade by The Ingram Book Company

Table of Contents

Prologue ix

Quadrant Leadership
in Sixty Seconds 1

Part One
The Brand Builders 7

Part Two
Finding Salvation 25

Part Three
Transitioning to Quadrant Leadership 75

Part Four
The Four Quadrants 111

Part Five
Lessons Learned Along the Way 203

A boss who insists on holding on to control, and a well-run business that is fully under control, are rarely in the same location.

This book is dedicated to the memory of
Evan Lovelace and Chad Manson,
two extraordinary young men who left
an indelible mark on my life. Gone too soon,
they inspire me to write my story.

Prologue

Two days later, I am back in Vancouver and ready to begin my seventh session. I am looking forward to sharing my Anaheim experience with this man who has become my most trusted ally. Even though I am extremely proud of what I was able to accomplish, I can no longer deny the fact that something is seriously wrong. When I look up, he is staring out the window his thoughts a million miles away. Suddenly, he stands and gently places his hand on my shoulder. As he looks into my eyes, my heart begins to race. In this critical moment I have no idea what he is about to say, but somehow I know it is going to change my life.

(Excerpt from *'Of Darkness and Light.'*)

No one can predict the future, and sometimes bad things happen to good people. What might have marked the end of my professional career with one of the most iconic companies in the world would lead instead to something truly remarkable.

This is the story of Quadrant Leadership.

All of the content, templates, terms of reference, and personal anecdotes contained in this book are the sole property of the author. Any reference to previously published or trademarked material is clearly acknowledged.

Quadrant Leadership
in Sixty Seconds

Every boss, no matter their vocation, is in the business of people.

The principles that lay at the heart of Quadrant Leadership are driven by one simple premise. 'The more people know, the more they are able to contribute.' This is a philosophy of leadership that is firmly rooted in the power of human potential.

While the idea of providing enhanced development to improve employee performance is hardly an original concept, it is the things we share in Quadrant Leadership, and the way we go about sharing them, that allow us to achieve such extraordinary results. Let me offer a couple of specific examples from my own business.

Within six months of making a full transition into Quadrant Leadership, I was able to reduce employee turnover in my company by eighty percent. In an industry where high turnover is standard fare, I was then able to maintain those numbers for the entire decade that I ran my business.

When it came to the profitability of my company, the results were just as impressive. Within a few short weeks of implementing the Quadrant Leadership Model, I began to experience a marked improvement in the bottom line. By the end of my first full year of operation, my profit numbers had risen by more than twenty percent. In a chapter entitled *Business and the Bottom Line*, I will share with you how I improved my profit margins simply by teaching my employees how cash flows through a business and how their decisions impact it every single day.

There are many reasons to consider Quadrant Leadership. Here are four of the best:

- It offers a highly effective, results-driven alternative to the way you currently run your business.
- It provides every employee in your company with the kind of business education that will prepare them to contribute in a far more significant way.
- It promotes an environment where healthy, productive working relationships are formed based on mutual trust and respect.
- It maintains focus on the core objectives of your business that will yield the greatest return on investment.

You are about to read a great deal about employee development, but make no mistake; Quadrant Leadership is not some fancy training program. It is a philosophy of leadership that targets enriched employee development to create extraordinary brand identity.

In Quadrant Leadership, one of our most important objectives is to free ourselves from the endless cycle of repetitive direction that is the bane of most traditional leadership models. By making a significant commitment to the ongoing development of every employee, our goal is to raise the level of personal accountability that everyone is expected to bring to the table.

Let's take a quick sixty-second look at some of the concepts, principles, and strategies that are not only unique to Quadrant Leadership, but highly effective as well.

We begin with the **Universal Truths of Employment.** You will find them on page 134. I suggest that you take a quick look at them now.

One of the most important objectives of Quadrant Leadership is to build healthy working relationships based on mutual trust and respect. The Universal Truths are intended to be an honest reflection of what it means to take on the responsibilities associated with being employed. I believe that every employee who comes to work for your company, regardless of their previous experience, should be given the same opportunity. Many will tell you that they have never had this kind of talk with an employer. By establishing a clear set of expectations from the beginning, you ensure that your new employee gets off to an excellent start.

Part III of the book is dedicated to preparing you for a successful transition into Quadrant Leadership. A critical first step in that process is determining how you currently use your time. We accomplish this task with a tool called the **Transition Journal**.

This interesting exercise serves to illustrate the important difference between perception and reality. You may think that recording the way you currently use your time is unnecessary because you already know the answer. Most people who complete the journal will tell you that it was a real eye opener. How we use the journal and the activities that we record in it can be found on page 87.

One of the most important steps in the transition phase involves familiarizing yourself with the **Quadrant Leadership Model**. This tool will be used as the platform for all employee development that will take place in your company. While the model itself is addressed in detail starting on page 78, this visual of the master template should give you a good idea of what is taking place. Let's look at it now.

Mutual Respect
The Foundation For All Healthy Relationships

Each of the quadrants that make up the model has its own master template. You will find them on pages 114, 128, 156 and 182, respectively.

Being able to approach a development opportunity from four different perspectives has the potential to enhance significantly the learning experience. The environment that you create for these sessions will play a critical role in the outcome. As your relationship with each employee continues to evolve, the level of respect that follows will allow you to increase your sphere of influence exponentially.

One of the many unique things we do in Quadrant Leadership is to explore the relationship between the way people naturally think and the way that they learn. We call this exercise **Detailed Thinkers Versus Concept Thinkers.** Armed with a better understanding of how an employee processes information, we are able to improve the quality of a training session dramatically. You can read more about this highly effective training tool beginning on page 121.

One of the most important subjects we approach in the Teacher/Philosopher Quadrant is the role that character can play in finding success, not only in business but also in life in general. For many companies, the only time the subject of character comes up is when it becomes an issue affecting the employee's performance. In Quadrant Leadership, our approach is to explore positive character traits that are common to successful people. In a chapter entitled **Character and Self-Reflection**, we look at how a discussion related to character can lead to a natural progression towards self-reflection. You will find this chapter on character building beginning on page 151.

Throughout the years that I continued to refine the Quadrant Leadership Model, I looked for ways to improve my coaching skills. There is a significant difference between teaching and coaching, and while both play an important role in the development process, good coaching skills are the catalyst to real change. In **The Art of Coaching**, I share with you five effective coaching strategies that can significantly improve employee performance. You will find those strategies beginning on page 160.

So many small business owners fail to understand the critical role that brand identity plays in building a successful small business. One of the reasons that the Quadrant Leadership Model is so effective is because it targets enhanced employee development to build strong brand identity. Every credible company that has ever stood the test of time has done so by adhering to the core values and guiding principles that define the essence of its brand. Brand identity is what distinguishes your business from your competitors in the eyes of the consumer. The single most important thing that you can do to build long-term market share is to create brand loyalty.

On page 19, you will find the master template for **The Brand Identity Model**. It is broken into Brand Integrity and Brand Recognition, the two critical components of every credible brand.

One of the most effective tools that we use in Quadrant Leadership can be found in a chapter called **Meetings Versus Power Briefings**. The objective of power briefings is to reduce drastically the number of meetings you attend or conduct with others. I have a low opinion of meetings and consider the majority of them to be a complete waste of time. Power briefings, on the other hand, are results-driven, quick, and easy communication sessions. You will find the chapter on power briefings beginning on page 206.

There are many things we do in Quadrant Leadership to promote employee productivity. One of the best examples is the way we approach **conditional praising**. Most employees consider a conditional praise to be insincere. Before they have a chance to feel good about the positive feedback they have just received, they are hit with something they need to improve upon. By separating the two parts of the conditional praise, the employee gets to enjoy the feelings associated with positive reinforcement, and you get to address the area of opportunity. The result is a win-win scenario. You will find the chapter on Praising Without Conditions starting on page 165.

Let's take a look at one more example. In Quadrant Leadership, we classify the valuable time you spend on activities that do little to improve your business as **busy-work.** Far too many bosses today are drowning in busy-work. I encourage you to take a look at some of the primary activities that fall under the busy-work umbrella on page 97. Some of them might surprise you.

When all is said and done, you may be tempted to cherry pick the things from Quadrant Leadership that appeal the most to you. While I have no doubt that your business would improve, you will miss an incredible opportunity to achieve some truly remarkable results. Like every credible example of synergy in motion, Quadrant Leadership is exponentially at its best when the sum of all its parts comes together as one.

I spent my entire corporate career employing a very traditional style of leadership. While I enjoyed a great deal of success, I consider the results I achieved in my own business embracing Quadrant Leadership to be far superior and more rewarding. If you are looking for fresh ideas that have the potential to take your business to a whole new level, you have come to the right place.

Part One
The Brand Builders

In Good Company   10

Brand Power   12

Life, Lemons, and Lemonade 22

In Good Company

"God has given us our talents, not to copy the talents of others, but rather to use our brains and imagination in order to obtain the revelation of true beauty."

– Louis Comfort Tiffany

When I first set out to explore the merits of Quadrant Leadership, I remembered a biography I had once read on Louis Comfort Tiffany. Most historians consider Tiffany to be the greatest artisan of the modern era. His name is synonymous with a level of quality that is beyond compare.

Tiffany was a genius and a great visionary; he was also an extraordinary teacher. No matter how famous he became or how big his company grew, he never abandoned his principle role as a master craftsman.

His creative mind allowed him to experiment in many different mediums, and he never grew tired of sharing his knowledge and insight with the talented men and women whose own works would carry his family namesake. Through his personal creations, he established a benchmark for what is possible when people strive to do their best. Throughout his life, he never lost sight of what made him successful, and he continued to show the way until the end.

As Tiffany's empire grew, it would have been easy for him to turn over this very important role to one of his most trusted artisans. Instead, he chose to remain on the front lines, inspiring others to hold themselves accountable to the same standards of excellence to which he aspired.

By never losing sight of the core values that solidified the status of his company, he established an extraordinary brand that has stood the test of time. Nearly a century after his death, Louis Comfort Tiffany's legacy lives on. If you have ever watched an episode of "Antiques Road Show", you will know that owning a vintage piece of Tiffany can be a very good investment.

If I learned one important lesson from his story, it is never to lose sight of the fundamentals that define your brand.

Every day, companies must battle for market share. Some will win, and some will lose. With Quadrant Leadership, our goal is to create an entire army of extraordinary brand builders dedicated to bringing the core values of our business to life in a very significant way. By demonstrating their true abilities, our employees inspire us to mold and to shape our business in ways we never imagined possible.

Brand Power

"The only place where success comes before work is in the dictionary."

– Vidal Sassoon

I have the greatest respect for entrepreneurs. These are the risk-takers and innovators, visionaries and dreamers, who contribute to the health and welfare of every small town and big city in a very substantial way. Through their vast network of small and mid-sized businesses, they create more jobs than all of big business and the government combined. These incredibly diverse, multi-faceted, free enterprise super engines are without question the lifeblood of the North American economy.

Several years ago, I was invited to speak at a symposium for start-up companies hosted by the Business Development Bank of Canada. At the time, I was head of Training and Employee Development for McDonald's Restaurants, Western Canada. The conference room was abuzz with entrepreneurs from every walk of life, young and old alike, eager to learn everything they could about what it takes to run a successful small business.

As the final speaker of the day, I began my presentation with a piece I had written several years earlier entitled 'Ode to the Entrepreneur.' As all eyes descended upon the content of a single page, excited chatter quickly gave way to total silence.

Ode to the Entrepreneur
'The Unsung Hero of Our Economy'

As the owner of a small business, you are beholden to many people:

Your banker, who holds your demand loan.

Your family and friends, who believed in you and invested in your success.

Your landlord and the obligations of your lease.

Your customers, who expect a great deal for their hard-earned money. They can be impossible to please and easily lured away. There is no such thing as guaranteed loyalty. You have to fight for their patronage every single day.

Your staff who can be your greatest asset and your biggest pain in the butt. Even though they do not share your burden or your worries, they are your salvation and the key to your success.

Your suppliers with their rising costs and demand payments, and those who service your company who always seem to charge a labor rate that makes you wish you were in their business instead of your own.

And, of course, there are the taxes: Property taxes and payroll taxes, small business and personal income taxes, sales taxes, user fees and municipal levies. It seems that every branch of the government looks to small business to solve their revenue shortfalls.

Then there's the time commitment. No forty-hour work week here. No weekends off. Small business men and women carry the burden of a thousand responsibilities. The livelihoods of so many people rest in their hands.

Many are the days these great titans of industry work for free, the price they pay for the privilege of ownership. Proprietors of their own destiny, every day they walk a tightrope called risk and reward, with no safety net below.

These brave men and women dare to risk everything they have to invest in not only their future but in our future as well. The significant contributions they make to creating jobs and sustaining a healthy economy for our community enrich our lives in so many ways.

I salute these incredible visionaries who dare to dream. They represent the very definition of free enterprise. And if a few of the luckier ones happen to make a million bucks along the way, we should stand and applaud, for they have earned every penny.

***

When I originally wrote the piece, it was intended as an homage to the entrepreneurial spirit. For this particular group, just beginning their journey, it served as a sober reminder that the road ahead would be anything but easy.

In preparing for my presentation, I made the conscious decision to focus my comments on the real challenges that lay ahead for the majority of these entrepreneurs. While it was not my intention to cause alarm, I knew that based on statistics alone, there would be many casualties along the way. I felt it incumbent upon myself to offer insight on the things that I believed would help them to assess the health of their business at any given time.

I surprised my fellow presenters by opening with bankruptcy statistics for first-year small business, and the short window that a company has to become established. I made it clear that without positive cash flow, a business would quickly find itself in trouble. I talked about having realistic sales goals and the relationship between the top and bottom line. In addressing the profit and loss statement, I targeted the controllable section in particular, emphasizing the importance of minimizing the impact of fixed costs while effectively managing every single variable cost that the business incurred.

When I stopped to take a sip of water, it was clear that I had captured their undivided attention. The room was so quiet I could actually hear myself swallow. As a presenter, I am not used to standing behind a podium. I find it seriously limits my ability to communicate. Since I was about to deliver my most important message of the day, I freed the mike from the dais and stepped off the stage and into the crowd. I wanted to make direct eye contact with as many of these entrepreneurs as possible. It was important that they listened carefully to what I was about to say next.

I prefaced my comments by saying, "If you take nothing else away from what I have shared with you today, please remember this:

"Nothing will play a greater role in the long-term success of your business than your ability to create your own unique brand identity. The core values and guiding principles that will define your brand are not a wish list; they are a must list."

I paused just long enough to let my words sink in and then I repeated them before carrying on.

"Your brand identity is who you are and what you stand for. It is your footprint, your signature, your calling card. It is what your reputation will be built upon and how you will be measured. Most importantly, your brand is what sets you apart from all of your competitors in the eyes of the consumer.

As heads began to nod, I could feel the connection being made.

"Advertising campaigns and marketing strategies will help to build brand awareness for your business, but it is your ability to deliver the goods, what we call your brand integrity, that will ultimately determine your success. If you are able to live up consistently to the promises of your brand, you will earn the kind of customer loyalty that is critical to building long-term market share.

"Every small business owner must look at themselves as the steward of their brand. In the end, it's not your words that will make the difference, but what you do with them."

As I was drawing to a close, I could see many tired faces. I had no doubt that many of these entrepreneurs were already putting in an enormous number of hours. The risk for burnout was very real, and so my final comments were centered on the importance of building a solid team. I reminded them of what I had said in Ode to the Entrepreneur about their employees. *'Even though they do not share your burden or your worries, they are your salvation and the key to your success.'*

As I turned to take my seat, I received the first standing ovation of the day. It took me by complete surprise, considering the content of my presentation. Our host returned to the podium and thanked all four presenters for a fantastic day. We stood in unison as the audience rose once more to show their genuine appreciation.

As the other presenters were leaving the stage, I began to return notes to my briefcase. Before I could finish, I found myself surrounded. As I contemplated the best way to handle the situation, our host came to my rescue and requested that everyone take a seat. It took a few seconds for me to realize that the majority of the audience had remained behind. Over the next hour and a half, I fielded numerous questions until finally the banquet manager requested we wrap things up so that his people could prepare the room for an evening event.

On my drive home, I began to reflect on the events of the day. I was satisfied that I had done a credible job of addressing the majority of their questions, but it was obvious that we had barely begun to scratch the surface.

***

Long before most corporations recognized the importance of community involvement, McDonald's was leading the way. A perfect example was the pilot project that came about as a result of that impromptu question and answer session. I saw an opportunity for McDonald's to provide a slightly different kind of community support. The rationale behind my proposal was that a strong and vibrant small business network was good for everyone, including McDonald's. With the blessing of my bosses and the full support of the Business Development Bank, I put together a series of workshops for local entrepreneurs. For the next three months, I conducted one session per week to a capacity crowd. Within a matter of weeks, it became necessary to limit the number of sessions that each entrepreneur could attend before placing their name on the wait list.

Even though there was a tremendous amount of work involved, I thoroughly enjoyed the entire experience. I met many interesting people and gained tremendous respect for the level of interest they brought to each session. Many years later, when I was creating the Quadrant Leadership Model, I drew heavily on the important lessons I learned while conducting those workshops.

Some of the most popular sessions addressed hard numbers, including managing cash flow, calculating break-even sales, and analyzing profit and loss statements. While I would continue to include these types of topics in future sessions, I knew that if the cash registers were not ringing, none of these things would matter.

Session three began with the four statements that appear on the back of the book cover. They would remain on display at the front of the room for the duration of the project.

> Every day companies must compete for market share. The only way to grow your business is to take market share away from someone else.
>
> The core values and guiding principles that are the cornerstone of every successful small business are not a wish list; they are a 'must list'.
>
> The three most over used, yet seldom achieved words in the business vernacular are 'Total Customer Satisfaction.'
>
> Nothing will ever be more important to the long-term success of your business than your ability to create brand equity.

It was my habit to begin each workshop with a story that had some relevance to the topic at hand. In this case, I needed the connection to be far more personal, so I selected an exercise instead. Everyone in the room was asked to close their eyes and visualize a commercial street in their neighborhood lined with several small businesses. I asked them to begin at one street corner and write down the names of each business in order. Once they arrived at the next corner, they were to cross the street and continue down the other side. If they were not able to recall the name of a business, they should try to indicate what type of business it was.

I have done this exercise many times over the years, and the results are almost always the same. Save for a handful of people with photographic memories, most people have many blank spaces on their piece of paper.

It will not surprise you to learn that the businesses located on street corners were the easiest to remember. Prime location offers two distinct advantages. The first is convenience with ease of access, and the second is unrestricted visibility with strong recall presence. Customers rate both of these attributes extremely high when it comes to making quick decisions. There is no question that a business that can take full advantage of the exposure it receives from strategic location has a decided edge over its competition.

Since most businesses do not enjoy the good fortune of being in the best locations, the most powerful weapon in their arsenal is their brand identity. In the fierce battle for market share, reputation is key. Market share is a reflection of consumer choice, which is directly influenced by the customer's perception of the brand.

The memory exercise was meant to illustrate the importance of creating a strong brand identity. Despite the fact that thousands of potential customers walk past their doors every single day, for many of these businesses, their inability to create a lasting impression in the minds of the consumer left them virtually invisible.

While brand development may seem like an abstract concept, it is actually a straightforward process. The starting point will differ slightly for someone who is inheriting an existing brand compared to someone starting from scratch, but the principles are the same. In both cases, the key to optimizing the potential power of the brand rests in the hands of the entrepreneur. Let's take a look at the model.

BRAND IDENTITY

Brand Integrity

Principles and Values

The guiding principles and core values that the company's business model is built upon

Expectations

Set of pledges, commitments and promises that a company makes to it's customers

Execution

The company's ability to deliver on promises made

Brand Recognition

Awareness

The immediate connection between a company's name, logo or website and the goods and services it provides

Reach

The size of the trading area where the brand enjoys a high degree of recognition

Reputation

Consumer perception that drives brand loyalty

Brand Equity

The good will value of the brand based on the company's performance over a sustained period of time

Before we go any further, I'd like to clear up an important misconception. I was surprised to learn that many of the entrepreneurs who came to my workshops had the impression that brand identity was somehow reserved as the exclusive domain of large corporations. Nothing could be further from the truth. All you need to do is look at the local businesses in your community that have made a significant name for themselves. By consistently delivering on the core values of their brand, they are able to grow market share through one of the most powerful forms of advertising that every business has at its disposal: *Word of mouth*.

If you want proof of what brand equity can cost, just ask someone who has purchased a franchise from a reputable company with strong brand identity, or a well-established local business with a long history of consistent sales and healthy profits.

While there are many advantages to purchasing either of these kinds of businesses, it would be a mistake to believe that your work is done. The halo effect that comes with acquiring an existing company will quickly lose its luster if you rely solely on brand recognition.

Creating the kind of brand integrity that makes you a real contender requires serious commitment. You must be able to earn both the trust and the confidence of your customers. If you fail to deliver on the promises of your brand, they will look for alternatives. In the end, companies that are able to build consumer loyalty have the greatest opportunity to grow their market share.

***

One of the things I enjoyed the most about those workshops was the passion most of the entrepreneurs had for their business. The biggest challenge they would face would be turning that passion into actionable words. The core set of values and guiding principles that define the essences of a reputable brand must ooze with substance. It is not the words that matter, but the actions they generate that define a brand's true integrity. From those values will come a set of commitments that your customers will come to rely on. In the end, it is your ability to deliver on promises made that will determine your success.

Throughout every session, I spent a great deal of time emphasizing the role that employee development would play in bringing their brand to life. While my advice was rock solid, it was not until I fully embraced the principles of Quadrant Leadership that I began to understand how people like Tiffany were able to create such a remarkable brand that none of his competitors were able to duplicate.

Life, Lemons, and Lemonade

Each of us will deal with a number of personal setbacks in our lifetime. For the most part, we weather through these challenging times with few consequences. For some people however, there are circumstances that are so profound that nothing is ever the same again. I know because I happen to be one of those people.

In the winter of 1991, I received a diagnosis that would drastically alter the course of my life. The great irony of my personal misfortune is that it would be the catalyst that would lead me to Quadrant Leadership. Faced with this new reality and a whole set of new challenges, I had no choice but to take stock of every aspect of my life, including how I viewed my role as a leader. If one of the qualities of a good leader is how they handle change, then the question I had to answer was, what was it going to take to manage profound change?

I love the art of storytelling. Whether I am addressing a large audience, conducting a small interactive workshop, or writing a book, the idea of entertaining while educating is something that greatly appeals to me. The next section, Finding Salvation, is a collection of three short stories that explore the evolution of my role as a leader, before and after my diagnosis.

The first story in the trilogy is called *The Taxman Cometh*. It offers some insight into how I used Quadrant Leadership to run my own business. The poor government auditor who braved a blustery autumn morning would leave completely baffled by his experience. He could not understand how a company could be running so well when the guy who was supposedly in charge seemed so completely inept.

In the first two stories, I get an opportunity to share my history with one of the most recognized and iconic companies in the world. I had the great pleasure to call McDonald's Restaurants my home, both as a corporate employee and later as a private entrepreneur for more than three decades. The remarkable business education I received during my tenure with this extraordinary company is something that could never be replicated in any classroom. It would serve me well as I transitioned into the world of free enterprise.

To be clear, the Entrepreneur's Apprentice is not a book about McDonalds or its trade secrets. All of the concepts, principles, and strategies that I share with you in this book are unique to Quadrant Leadership. While McDonald's provided me with an outstanding platform to build my business upon, by implementing Quadrant Leadership Model, I was able to outperform significantly, many of my contemporaries.

The last story in the trilogy is called *Of Darkness and Light*. This is my most personal story and by far the most difficult to write. I wrote it for three reasons. The first was that it was an incredibly cathartic experience. In reliving the darkest period of my life and what I was able to accomplish in all of the turbulence, I feel an enormous sense of pride. When I think back on those days now, it is hard to believe that I had both the wisdom and the fortitude to recognize the potential of Quadrant Leadership. The second reason, I have already alluded to. I feel comfortable in saying that had my life not taken such an unexpected turn, there would have been no major motivation to alter drastically my leadership style, and the extraordinary benefits of this remarkable way of running a small business would never have come to fruition. The third reason was purely personal. As an educator, I think that anytime you have an opportunity to shed some light on a subject that most people know little about, one that many feel uncomfortable talking about, then you should never pass up the chance.

Before I leave this chapter, I want to assure you that I have not lost sight of the fact that you picked up this book in search of credible tools to improve your business. The good news is that you have come to the right place. If time is of the essence, I encourage you to skip directly to *Transitioning to Quadrant Leadership* and get started.

When I think of the extraordinary results that I was able to achieve with Quadrant Leadership despite my personal challenges, I feel extremely optimistic about the prospects for your business.

Part Two
Finding Salvation

The Taxman Cometh	28
Driven	45
Of Darkness and Light	51

Salvation - noun
the preservation or deliverance from harm, ruin, or loss

The Taxman Cometh

Vancouver, British Columbia
November 4, 1995

4:45 a.m.

My God, what a storm. In all the years I've lived on the West Coast, I can honestly say I have never encountered anything like this. Gale force winds spun far out in the Pacific Ocean have slammed head-on into heavy rainfall. The result is a weather phenomenon that is far more powerful than anything we have experienced in decades. Several municipalities are reporting power outages, and for the first time in many years, the Fraser River is on flood alert.

As morning commuters wake to the latest news, law enforcement and city officials plead with the public to stay off the roads. I would like nothing more than to oblige, but there are circumstances in play that make it imperative that I get to Vancouver. My sense of urgency can be summed up in two unsettling words: Revenue Canada.

Several weeks ago, a registered letter arrived from the federal government informing me that my business had been 'selected for review.' Last Monday, I received a follow-up phone call to confirm the date and time. We may be in the midst of one of the biggest storms on record, but it does nothing to alter the fact that the taxman is on his way.

As I enter the freeway, I am under siege. With the strength of a supersonic car wash hyped up on steroids, the assault is intense. Powerful crosswinds shake my car so violently that the vibrations cause my teeth to chatter. The wall of water that engulfs my windshield is unforgiving and quickly overwhelms my wipers. For my safety, I have no choice but to reduce my speed and turn my full attention to the iridescent road reflectors that will be my only guide. For the life of me, I can't understand why he chose to start this thing so damned early.

As I enter the perimeter of the city, the storm shows no sign of abating. A quick glance at the time confirms that nearly an hour has passed. I slow down to catch the rhythm of the traffic lights and sail uncontested through the empty streets. With a little luck, I will be a few minutes early. What a relief.

As I turn the corner and enter the parking lot, my eyes are immediately drawn to the silhouette of a dark sedan. Headlights on. Engine idling. Wipers on intermittent. I wonder how long he has been waiting.

***

June 11, 1970

A week from today I will turn sixteen. As I stand in the garden of our little house on 59th street, I am deep in thought. For as long as I can remember, I have always been interested in landscape design. Today I have decided that I will add a fishpond to the front yard. I am just about to draw out a rough sketch when I hear my mother call. Perfect timing! I will ask for a couple of koi for my birthday present.

I am about to make my request when she hands me a copy of the local paper folded to an inside page.

"What?" I ask.

"There on the right, near the bottom."

My eyes scan down to a brief article, the headline caption in bold letters.

McDonald's Restaurants to Hire Twenty New Crew

In 1970, McDonald's is in its infancy in Canada. Barely three years old, the first restaurants are concentrated in a hand full of cities spread out across the country. The majority of Canadians have yet to experience their first taste of a Big Mac. In Vancouver, there are only two locations, units as we called them back then, with five in total in the Lower Mainland. The first restaurant in the country opened in Richmond, British Columbia, in June of 1967.

These early locations have little seating. With just a handful of outside patio tables, most customers eat in their cars. The building design is unique and immediately draws your attention. A prominent feature of the architecture is a set of large neon arches that rise high above the roofline. At night, they glow a bright yellow and are clearly visible in the distance. The term "Golden Arches" will soon become part of the Canadian vernacular. Parking spaces hug the building envelope. It will be another decade before the first drive-thrus appear on the scene. Advertising is primarily a local affair, mostly radio spots supported by a handful of national television commercials.

These early productions might be considered primitive by today's standards, but they quickly find an audience and are long remembered for their iconic jingles. "You deserve a break today, so get up and get away to McDonald's," is a classic of the early 1970s. It's also important to note that this is a time long before mega-malls and big box stores. Steady work for a young teenager is not easy to come by. Grocery store baggers, gas station and theater attendants, newspaper delivery boys, and the odd job cleaning up a lumberyard account for the majority of part-time employment options.

"Why are you showing me this?" I ask, hoping to sound confused.

"You need to get a job, and this sounds like the perfect opportunity."

To tell the truth, I'm not the least bit surprised. Part-time employment has become a regular topic around our dinner table. My parents, now deceased, were wonderful people. Hard-working, salt of the earth type folk who set the bar high when it came to work ethic.

Hoping to derail the discussion, or, at least, put it off for another day, I say, "Mom, I'm only fifteen. I thought you needed to be at least sixteen years old and have one of those social insurance cards before you could apply for a job." My hope is that a recitation of the facts will end the discussion.

"This is true," she counters. "Fortunately for us, you will be sixteen in just a few days. As far as the other matter goes, I have some more good news. Two months ago, I sent away for your very own card, and it arrived yesterday. It would appear that you have everything you need."

Before I have a chance to react, she reaches into her purse and presents me with a white, wallet-sized plastic card. Prominently displayed on the front are a series of embossed letters, my name in full, and a nine-digit number.

"Now put that in your wallet for safe keeping. You will need it next week when you fill out your application."

I feel numb. My mind is racing as I struggle to understand what is happening here.

"Donny," she repeats for the third time. "Are you okay?"

Realizing the impact her words have had on me, she steps forward and gives me a reassuring hug. She strokes my hair before continuing in a softer tone.

"You knew this day was coming, son. Truth be told, everybody has to start somewhere. Besides, I have a hunch you're going to like earning your own money."

That catches my attention.

"I have to admit, that part does sound pretty good."

"Of course, we can't get too far ahead of ourselves. First you have to get the job. Filling out the application will be the easy part. The important thing is impressing the interviewer when it's your turn in the hot seat. I'll tell you what, starting tonight, your Dad and I will help you practice."

"Dad?"

"Well okay, I'll help you practice, and your Dad can add in his two cents when he feels like it."

With the employment discussion concluded, she turns the conversation to my upcoming birthday.

"Now, have you given any thought to what you would like for your present this year?"

"A six-month reprieve from this job hunting thing sounds like a pretty good gift right about now."

Clearly not impressed with my answer, she says, "Why don't you try that again?"

"Okay then, how about fish?"

"I'm sorry, did you say fish?"

I nod. "Yes, I'd like a couple of really big koi."

"Aren't those outdoor fish?"

Before I answer, I glance at the wall clock. Today's conversation has put a serious wrench into my summer plans.

"They sure are. Now if you don't mind, Mom, I need to get going."

Still puzzled, she looks for clarification. "Where do you plan to keep these fish?"

"In the pond."

"What pond are you talking about?"

"Exactly!"

Before she has a chance to ask any more questions, I am off to the garden shed. As I turn the corner, I hear her say, "Well, if it's fish that the boy wants, it's fish he shall have." I smile to myself and yell, "Thanks, Mom!"

On July 3rd, 1970, I officially became the newest member of the Southwest Marine Drive McDonald's Crew, Unit # 8002. The final digit signified the second restaurant built in Canada. Ironically, that day would be the first and only time I would ever use my social insurance card to apply for a job for the next thirty-two years. I could never have imagined then that McDonald's would become my life-long career, or that the company would enter into the most explosive growth period in its history. It was an extraordinary time that would ultimately afford me many unique opportunities and experiences. I would make many mistakes along the way, but I would also stumble upon something quite remarkable.

***

As I step out of my car, I get my first real sense of the sheer intensity of the storm. In the distance I hear the crackle of power lines and wonder if today's meeting is all for not. Approaching the other vehicle, I tap my keys lightly on the driver's side window. The man inside jumps, startled by the abrupt interruption. I try to suppress a smile. This may be the only time today that I will find anything remotely amusing. According to the digital display on his dashboard, it is now 5:56 a.m. He turns off his interior light and returns files to his briefcase, paperwork no doubt for today's inquisition.

Opening his door, he rises quickly, and we exchange a perfunctory handshake. Official introductions will have to wait as we race to escape the onslaught of the storm.

The entrance to the building has a small overhang that will serve as our temporary refuge. As he waits for me to unlock the door, I scan the entire length of the dining room for any sign of movement. With no one in sight I bang the palm of my hand firmly on the glass door. From the corner of my eye, I see his head snap to attention.

With genuine confusion he asks, "Why don't you just use your key?"

I turn to face him before I reply. "Because I don't have one."

"You mean you forgot it?" he suggests, looking for clarification.

"No, I mean I don't have a key."

As he carefully considers my response, a prominent worry line begins to form across his brow. Before he has an opportunity to ask any further questions, I return to the task at hand. With both fists clenched tight, I vigorously assault the solid metal door frame. It makes such a racket that I am convinced that it can't be ignored.

As we stand in awkward silence, I close my eyes and concentrate on the haunting cadence of the wind. It has a hypnotic quality that sets my mind to wander. As I consider the bizarre events of the day so far, I can't help but reflect on the decision that brought me to this moment.

***

Fall, 1993

It is late October, and the lingering Indian summer is now on borrowed time. I'm about to begin my tour of our restaurants on the North Shore when my phone rings. It is my secretary and, judging from the tone of her voice, something is up.

"They're looking for you." 'They' are the vice president and the executive vice president of the company.

"Can you tell them that I should be able to get back to the office in about twenty minutes?"

I turn on my ignition and enter the flow of traffic that will lead me to the Second Narrows Bridge. At this time of the day, it will be the fastest route back. Rolling down my window, I enjoy the warm breeze as it flows gently across my face. I need to remain calm and concentrate on taking deep breaths. This sudden bout of anxiety is precipitated by the fact that I know exactly why I have been summoned. It appears that they have finally made their decision.

As the operations manager for the Greater Vancouver Area, I am responsible for the sales, profits, and employee development of thirty-four restaurants. My patch has a compliment of five supervisors, one hundred and forty-eight full-time managers, and a crew roster numbering more than three thousand restaurant employees. With two more restaurants slated to open in December, this has been an exceptionally busy and demanding year.

In July, I celebrated my twenty-third year with McDonald's Restaurants of Canada. It seems hard to believe when you consider that I am only thirty-nine years old. I have literally grown up with this company. As I settle into the drive, I begin to reflect on the journey that has brought me this far. For the most part, the experience has been extremely gratifying. Of course, there have been incidents I wish I had dealt with differently, and a few decisions I truly regret, but overall I feel content. I have given my all and I feel ready for a change.

In August, I requested a meeting and expressed a strong desire to move on to a new chapter in my life. I stated my case and hoped that they would seriously consider my request. I was told that I would be notified when a decision had been reached. I'm nervous as I enter the parking lot, but it feels good. I tell myself that no matter what happens, I will survive. Beads of sweat roll down my back as I take one more deep breath. Reaching for my briefcase, I step out of my car.

I will not dwell on the details. In truth, it all happened so quickly that I barely remember who said what. What I do recall with great clarity is that I received the news I had longed to hear. My request would be granted. On January 1, 1994, I would officially become a McDonald's owner/operator, with my very own restaurant in Vancouver.

The days that followed became a crash course in preparing for life as a private entrepreneur. I would need a good lawyer, a good accountant and, of course, every penny I owned. The next few years would be lean, but I didn't care. I was so excited to get the chance to run my own company.

The time had come to implement critical changes in my leadership style. I knew there was a better way, and I was about to find out if I was up to the challenge. There would be no excuses, and no one else to blame should I fail. After all, I now owned the joint.[1]

***

I am drawn from my reverie by the sound of his voice.

"There's someone coming," he shouts excitedly.

As the door swings open, we scramble inside.

"Good morning, Teddy! How are you managing to cope with the storm of the century?"

"Other than a few flickering lights, I'd say we are doing pretty well. Are you okay? I heard this terrible noise and thought the wind might have shattered a window."

"I'm fine. I'm afraid the racket was all me. I was trying to grab your attention."

He chuckles and nods with a smile. "You definitely did that. Is there anything else you need before I get back to work?"

"No, we're good. I can take it from here. Thanks for coming to our rescue."

As Teddy walks away, I turn my attention back to the man who is responsible for today's meeting. He is tall and slender, with broad shoulders and jet-black hair. With his dark-framed glasses in place, he bears a striking resemblance to Clark Kent, Superman's alter ego. As he hands me the last of his rain-soaked gear, I invite him to take a seat.

"Would you care for a cup of coffee," I ask?

"Yes please, that would be great."

"Let me get these things hung up and I will meet you back here in a few minutes. Please make yourself comfortable."

---

[1] The expression 'I own the joint' was one that I would use on specific occasions. When faced with an unruly customer whose conduct or verbal diatribe was completely unacceptable, I often employed the phrase. These disgruntled patrons would usually argue that I had no right to ask them to leave. In response I would always say, "I am afraid that is where you are dead wrong. You see, I own the joint."

I am on my way back up the stairs when I spot one of my two regular breakfast staff.

"Hey, Noralyn. Glad to see you made it in one piece. Can you believe this weather? It reminds me of that scene in *The Wizard of Oz*."

"I know what you mean. That wind is totally insane. I had to ditch my umbrella and run the whole way."

She pauses momentarily when she suddenly realizes who she is talking to. "What on earth are you doing here at this hour?"

Instead of answering her question, I make a request.

"Could you please fire up the coffee machine for me?"

"Sure, but you don't drink coffee."

"Oh, it's not for me, it's for my guest in the lobby."

"There's someone sitting in the dining room? At this hour? Are you kidding me?"

"I wish I were. Listen, I promise to tell you all about it later. Right now, we need to make coffee."

"I'll get right on it. It should only take a couple of minutes. By the way, have you walked past a mirror lately? You look like a drowned rat."

I attempt to catch a glimpse of myself in the stainless steel on the side of the shake machine, but the image is blurred. Probably a good thing.

"Don't worry," I tell her. "I'll pretty up before we open."

Just then, I spot Jinky setting up the front counter area. As I catch her attention, she waves, and I realize something is off. I wave back and then turn to Noralyn.

"Hey, where's Robyn?"

"Oh, she had to give her husband a ride to work. Apparently, he was not able to get his car started this morning. Something about the distributor cap being too wet. She should be here by 6:30. I was able to get Jinky to cover for her.

I pause and smile. "Now that's funny."

"What is?"

"What you just said."

"I'm sorry, I don't follow. "

"Think about it. If the motto of the postal service is 'neither snow nor rain nor heat nor gloom of night can keep the postman from delivering the mail,' then why is it that my breakfast manager has to deliver the postman to the post office?"

"Oh brother, is that the best you've got?"

"It is at six in the morning."

I turn my attention back to the work at hand.

"Will you guys be okay?"

"Sure, Jinky and I have everything covered. Robyn will have plenty of time to get caught up.

"Sounds good to me."

Glancing over at the coffee machine, I see that the brew cycle has finished.

"Would you please deliver an extra large cup out to our friend and let him know that I will be along shortly? Right now, I need to make a phone call."

On the seventh ring, I hang up. Mike, my restaurant manager, has obviously assessed the situation and decided to head in early. Now that the rush hour is underway, his commute is likely to be much worse than mine. I just hope he's okay. Nothing is worth risking your personal safety for, least of all a government audit. When I return to the lobby, my guest is systematically laying out an array of paperwork. My eyes widen as I contemplate the ordeal that lies ahead. As I approach, he turns, and we finally have an opportunity to exchange proper introductions. He thanks me for agreeing to meet him so early. Agreeing? I didn't realize I had a choice

It turns out that he and his wife are scheduled to leave for a long overdue Hawaiian vacation later this afternoon. His goal is to have the audit completed well before the noon hour. I assure him that we will do everything in our power to get him out of here on time. As I look out the window, I wonder if it has occurred to him that the airport is likely closed. Maybe he'll get lucky, and things will clear up. Right now, that is a big maybe. I decide not to bring it to his attention.

The plan for today has been in place for several weeks. My job is to break the ice and get an idea of what to expect. Judging from the stack of paperwork, I would say a hell of a lot. Mike and Raheesh, one of my second assistant managers, will work directly with the auditor. They are both expected to arrive around seven o'clock. Fortunately, Raheesh lives close by and should have no trouble getting here. We will have to wait and see how Mike fares.

My first McDonald's restaurant is located on the east side of the city at the corner of Main Street and 29th Avenue. It is one of only a handful of leased sites. When I was the head of the Training Department for Western Canada, one of my favorite responsibilities was to speak on behalf of the corporation at various functions. Many people were surprised to learn that McDonald's is one of the largest holders of commercial real estate in the world.

The principle of acquiring the land and then constructing a restaurant on it can be traced back to McDonald's early days in the United States. The practice is credited to Harry Sonneborn, who became the company's first president. He was one of the early pioneers recruited by Ray Kroc, founder of McDonald's Restaurants, to rapidly expand the company. Sonneborn's franchising strategy is considered a critical cornerstone in the McDonald's success story.

Unlike many competitors, who are beholden to landlord demands and escalating lease costs, McDonald's is primarily exempt from these issues by maintaining ownership of the majority of its properties.

My location on Main Street is an exception to the rule and initially opened as a Safeway before becoming a McDonald's. As part of my purchase agreement, the restaurant underwent a major renovation. With two hundred and forty seats and full-size kids playroom, it is one of the largest non-drive-through locations in the city.

"How's the coffee?" I ask.

"Incredibly good."

"You seem surprised."

"Ah, well, you know, I mean no offense, but it's McDonald's coffee."

"You might be interested in learning that McDonald's quality standards require that our suppliers use only the finest coffee beans available, to produce a custom blend that is comparable to anything you will find in any of the upscale restaurants in the city."

"You're kidding, right?"

"Would I lie to you?"

"I am not sure that is a question you want to ask an auditor."

"Good point. I guess you'll just have to take my word for it. I have no idea what time you got up this morning, but I suspect that you are starting to get hungry. Once we are ready to open for business, I'll have my staff prepare you some breakfast. In case you were wondering, the answer is real eggs, and yes, they are grade A."

He smiles and says, "I suppose I had that one coming. I will say this; if it is half as good as this coffee, I look forward to it." A quick glance at his watch and his attention returns back to the task at hand.

"My goodness, look at the time. We really need to get going."

"No problem," I say. "I have assigned two of my managers to take part in the audit today. I expect them to arrive any minute now."

"That's not a problem, but I don't want to risk falling behind so how about if we get started, and they can join us as soon as they get here?"

It is clear that I cannot stall him any longer.

"All right then, where would you like to begin?

"Well, since you are still closed, I think a good place to start would be with your safe controls. Where is your safe located?"

He waits for me to lead the way, but instead I head toward the front doors. As I peer out into the driving rain, I hear him approach.

"Are you expecting someone else?"

"Yes, my breakfast manager, Robyn."

"Is she one of the managers who will be joining us on the audit this morning?"

"No, but we can't open the safe without her."

He pauses momentarily, wondering if he has heard me correctly.

"Come again?"

"We need Robyn to open the safe. "

"Are you trying to tell me that you do not know the combination to your own safe?"

"I'm afraid so."

His face takes on a pained expression as he places his paperwork on a nearby table. Removing his glasses, he pinches the bridge of his nose. When he speaks, there is a noticeable shift in his tone.

"Let me see if I've got this straight. First you tell me that you have no keys to open the front door, leaving the two of us stranded in the pouring rain. Now you are telling me that you have no idea what the combination to the safe is. Have I got that right?

At this point, my instincts tell me to let him vent so I remain silent and simply nod. As he continues, his voice begins to rise slowly with each measured syllable.

"This is your business, is it not? I mean, you are the owner of this McDonald's restaurant, are you not?"

Again, I nod. He is now shaking his head in total dismay and can no longer contain his frustration.

"I am at a total loss here. I really don't understand what is going on. All I can say is that this is one hell of a way to run a business."

I want to reassure him that his concerns are for naught, but instead, I continue to elevate his exasperation when I say, "Did you know that Albert Einstein never knew his own phone number? He believed that you should keep your mind free to concentrate on matters of real importance, rather than on the kinds of things that are easily accessible through other means."

"What on earth has that got to do with having a set of keys or a safe combination?"

"Nothing, I suppose." I pause. "And yet, everything."

He stares at me in total bewilderment. I am about to attempt an explanation when I detect movement in the background. Without any warning, I simply shout, "Reprieve," releasing a sea of pent-up tension.

My outburst startles him, and he takes a step backward, tripping over several chairs. Fortunately, I am able to grab his arm, avoiding a full-on fall. He regains his composure as I nod in the direction of the front doors.

"It would seem our safe problem is solved. My breakfast manager has just arrived." I smile as Robyn approaches.

"Good morning. I see you managed to deliver the postman safely to his destination."

"I can tell that you've been talking to Noralyn. We had no idea his car wouldn't start."

"No worries, they've got you covered."

She stares at the pile of paperwork spread out before her and says, "Wow, it looks like you guys have got a ton of work to do. How's it going so far?"

Before I respond, I check my peripheral vision. I can see that the auditor is looking directly at me. With a broad smile on my face, I turn and say, "Well, we just got started, but I would say it's going great."

His eyes widen, but before he can say a word, I turn my attention back to Robyn.

"Listen, would you do me a favor and open the safe? We need to count the contents before the tills go up this morning."

"Sure, I'll do it right now."

As Robyn makes her way towards the kitchen, I turn my attention back to the auditor and simply say, "Well, shall we get started?

Our first task is barely underway when I hear two familiar voices. It appears both of my salaried managers have arrived safe and sound. I feel a genuine sense of relief. They are comparing horror stories about the weather that I have no doubt will be told several times today. Right now, however, we have more important matters to attend to. As they wave in my direction, I wave back and point towards the lobby. I turn to the auditor and say, "I know you're anxious to get this thing started, but I would appreciate it if we could have a very short meeting, now that the rest of my team has arrived."

Reluctantly he agrees but makes me promise to keep it brief. I assure him that will not be a problem.

With everyone seated, I take the opportunity to introduce my managers and give the auditor some background on each of them. I explain the time constraints we are under and ask the guys to be prepared to expedite any requests as quickly and efficiently as possible. This last comment draws his attention and he says, "You make it sound like you won't be joining us."

"That's because I won't be joining you."

Before he can object, I continue. "I want you to know that both of these gentlemen are extremely knowledgeable and have access to all of the information you will require to complete your audit. If there is something that requires my attention, I will be right here working with the rest of my staff."

He is clearly unimpressed, and his body language makes no effort to hide his dissatisfaction. Resigning himself to the task, he slowly rises, and the three of them make their way toward the safe. At least, I have managed to keep his mind off the fact that there likely will be no flight to Hawaii today.

I would love to set him at ease, but a little piece of me is enjoying this immensely. Usually, it is the poor guy being audited who is doing the squirming. It is nice to see the shoe on the other foot for a change. I decide to let him discover on his own what I already know.

I won't bore you with the details of the audit. Suffice to say that when he approached me at 11:15 to review his findings, he had a genuine smile on his face.

***

Who knows why some memories stand out in our minds? For me, the events of that day remain crystal clear. The storm certainly added drama to the day, but it was his closing comments on the last page of the report that clearly captured the essence of Quadrant Leadership. Here is what was written, verbatim.

"The business practices of Steter Enterprises are exemplary. This is a very well-run company that owes its success to a very competent staff. How that came to be remains a total mystery to me. The one thing I can say with certainty is that Mr. Darvill is fortunate to have such a talented team of people working for him."

Years later when I was finally permitted to throw out the mountains of paperwork that one acquires as part of operating a small business, I mistakenly destroyed the only copy I had of that audit. When I began writing this story, I knew I would have no trouble recalling those words. Whenever I would find myself struggling with some aspect of this new approach to leadership, I would remember his words. They never failed to reassure me, or to make me smile.

I would never suggest that I have all of the answers and no approach to running a business is perfect. If my experience has taught me anything, it is that when you dedicate your time to the ongoing development of your people, amazing things begin to happen. The more they know, the more they truly can contribute. A highly skilled and empowered workforce is a formidable entity that is not easily defeated. The primary reason is simple: their pride of ownership will never let it happen.

Driven

I admire great leaders. They are steadfast in their pursuit of excellence. They innovate while staying true to core values. They influence through clarity of purpose and stand on the front lines of accountability. There is an air of confidence about them, a sense of total connection with what is real. They are the gatekeepers of all standards and practices, and will accept nothing less. They are the problem solvers, and more often than not, the final approval. They do not watch clocks and seldom work a forty-hour work week. Most of all, they are driven to succeed.

For the first twenty years of my career, this is exactly how I would have defined a great leader, and it is the kind of leader I strived to be. I was most definitely driven, and I set the bar high for myself, and for my people. I had little tolerance for poor work ethic and was never afraid to address the issue. I could be a tough boss, particularly when it came to maintaining standards. The importance of never compromising on the most important core values is something I learned early on in my career.

In 1974, when I was a young man, I had the good fortune to meet Ray Kroc, the founder of McDonald's Restaurants. The exchange, while brief, was one that I will never forget. That day I got the opportunity to watch a true master at work. I witnessed first-hand his relentless passion for the company he had built, and I listened carefully to his message.

For anyone interested in reading more about this extraordinary man, I recommend *Grinding It Out: The Making of McDonald's*, a fascinating read written in collaboration with Robert Anderson.

Ray had come up to Vancouver to visit his friend Ron Marcoux, the executive vice president for McDonald's Restaurants Western Canada. Part of his visit would be a tour of the McDonald's restaurants in the Greater Vancouver Area. At the time of Ray's visit, the Vancouver market had a solid reputation as one of the best-run McDonald's operations in North America. With Ron at the helm, Western Canada was also becoming known as a major innovator in new building design. One of the restaurants high on the priority list for Ray to see was our brand new location in the city of Richmond, just outside Vancouver.

This was the site of the first McDonald's restaurant ever built in Canada and a classic example of the original iconic design. Ron would often describe it to our young managers as "this funky little red and white building." With sleek lines, a reflection of the art deco period, it was a combination of tall glass windows, shiny red and white tiles, and two large neon arches that soared high above the roof line. The famous Golden Arches. To complete the design, an atrium inspired enclosure called the 'winter front' housed a handful of portable tables and chairs and protected the cash registers from inclement weather.

By comparison, the new restaurant that replaced the original was enormous and featured a brick facade that wrapped around the entire building. At nearly five times the size of the original red and white, the interior included two separate dining rooms, with enough seating for more than three hundred customers. This was in stark contrast to the original structure where the handful of seats that had once occupied valuable real estate in the winter front had been removed to make way for the sheer volume of customers who visited the tiny red and white restaurant every day.

As impressive as the inside of the new restaurant was, the real showstopper was the amazing outdoor kids play park. The building design called for floor to ceiling sliding doors off the west side dining room that could be opened to allow for full access to the park. Parents could sit in the comfort of the dining room while their children played out on the rock mountain or any one of the many McDonald's character rides. The craftsmanship of the mountain and rides was extraordinary. There was nothing else like it anywhere in the Greater Vancouver Area.

For a few brief weeks following the completion of the new restaurant, the two buildings stood side by side for the public to view. It was a symbol of just how far McDonald's Restaurants had come in such a short time in Canada.

I happened to be working at the little red and white during this transition period. Despite all of the headaches typically associated with a large construction project, we managed to keep the original restaurant open and operating at full capacity until the day of transition. I think many of the local residents in Richmond were feeling the nostalgia as well. Our final dinner hour was incredibly busy, and sales remained well above the norm right up until closing time. It was a special night for those of us who had been there from the beginning of the construction period. With the last customer served, we began the task of transferring the remaining food and operating supplies over to the new building in preparation for the first day of operations.

Ray Kroc's visit occurred a few weeks after the new location was up and running. He arrived at the restaurant surrounded by a large contingent of office personnel. Everyone, of course, was anxious to get his feedback on the design of the building, and the new kids play park.

Ray was obsessed with outstanding restaurant operations. He would describe it in a simple equation that consisted of just three letters: QSC. It stood for outstanding Quality, Service, and Cleanliness. In later years, the company would add a V to the equation to represent Value.

He answered their questions by asking a few of his own. How were we going to maintain the cleanliness standards in a building this large with a playground of that size? With ten cash registers, how would we maintain our service standards? He asked how a kitchen this size could be as efficient as the smaller, more streamlined version. I remember him turning to the group of office people and saying, "I want to talk to someone who runs this place. I want to hear what they have to say."

As circumstances would have it, our restaurant manager, Darryl McDougall, an extraordinary man and a great personal friend of mine, happened to be addressing a customer inquiry pertaining to the new playground. No one was prepared to keep Ray waiting, and so they turned to me. Fortunately, I was familiar with running the new restaurant and had just completed a training session for our staff on the transition. I did my best to tackle each of his questions. What I remember most about the encounter was how nervous I was.

The entire time I spoke, I remember that his eyes never left mine. As I addressed each of his concerns, he would nod, and when I was done, he thanked me for my input. He then proceeded to give his opinion of the new restaurant. I am of course paraphrasing here, but his message was clear. While addressing everyone, he looked directly at me.

"This is truly a beautiful building, son, that everyone involved in creating should be very proud of. Just remember that nothing is more important than QSC. If you always remember that, you will never fail. The minute you let other things get in the way, you will lose your advantage. Don't ever let the fancy stuff distract you from the things that really matter. Nothing, and I mean nothing, is more important than outstanding QSC."

No matter how often Ray Kroc spoke on McDonald's, his core message was always the same: QSC. He never grew tired of talking about it, and he firmly believed that for McDonald's to retain its edge and be successful in the future, we must never compromise our standards. Outstanding Quality, Service, and Cleanliness must always come before everything else. One of his favorite sayings was, "None of us is as good as all of us."

That day I understood why Ray Kroc was considered an iconic figure and a true leader in the industry. He refused to let anyone or anything get in the way of his message. The advice he gave me that day would stay with me for the rest of my life.

***

Finding success is one thing, but maintaining it is quite another. It is an enormous task that no one can accomplish on their own. Most bosses who embrace the traditional style of leadership surround themselves with a core team of people who play a critical role in the overall success of the company. These top performers are typically in positions of authority with the task of supervising or managing other employees. It can be an effective way to run a company, providing that your key players remain in place and maintain the level of excellence expected of them. Because this style of leadership relies so heavily on a highly developed core team, any disruption to the makeup or performance of that team can have immediate implications. These individuals are usually the driving force behind achieving the goals of the company. When any of them is missing or underperforming, it becomes a greater challenge to maintain excellence. By the time I was ready to take on a restaurant of my own, I had an idea for an entirely different way to lead, one that would challenge every employee to contribute more. Rather than relying on a small group of outstanding performers to carry the weight of accountability, this approach would focus on providing each employee with the kind of development that would capitalize on their potential to contribute more to the overall success of the company.

I had the great pleasure of working in the McDonald's Training Department for the better part of four years. It was a truly rewarding experience, and it gave me the opportunity to hone my skills as an effective communicator. The material we taught was first rate, and it provided our managers with the knowledge and tools to become great leaders in their own right.

Around this time, I began to ponder a concept that I would later come to call Quadrant Leadership. McDonald's is world-renowned for the quality of its training programs. These programs play an integral role in the company's enormous success. Topics like exploring the dynamics of winning teams and critical thinking for effective decision-making were instrumental in the development of our managers. I began to wonder what would happen if we were able to provide a higher level of personal development for every employee in the organization. Would it be worth the effort? Would the time invested lead to better employees? Would they, in turn, be inclined to contribute more to the success of the company? I had no idea what the answers were, but at the very least, it was an intriguing idea that I felt was worth pursuing.

Before I had the opportunity to explore the concept, I was promoted to the position of operations manager for the city of Vancouver. I was now responsible for the sales, profits, employee staffing, and operations of an entire urban region. With more than three thousand employees under my wing, I was about to experience the most demanding job of my corporate career.

From the beginning, my message was always the same: Nothing was more important than QSC, and nothing ever would be. Outstanding restaurant operations would be the key to our success. Every speech I made as an operations manager echoed the words of the man himself. Ray Kroc never grew tired of the message and neither would I. Getting there would definitely be a challenge, but the real work would be in maintaining a level of operational excellence that would set us far apart from our competition. No one knew better than Ray Kroc that when we are operating at the top of our game, no one can touch us.

I was just beginning to see some excellent results when a routine visit to the doctor would change everything.

Of Darkness and Light

Fall 1991

Today is Monday, and I have managed to clear enough from my calendar to free up the entire day. The summer months were incredibly busy, and now that fall has finally arrived, I have a little room to breathe. My biggest challenge since becoming an operations manager has been to find enough time to take care of basic chores around the house. The priority for today is to get the lawns cut. They are in dire need of my attention.

Since my divorce, I have struggled to find the delicate balance between the ever-present demands of my job and my new role as a single dad. Our custody agreement is not specific, but for now, the boys spend three of every four weekends with me. It has not been an easy transition, but we do the best we can. Despite our disagreements, my ex-wife and I are both determined to place the welfare of our children above all else.

More than anything, I just want our lives to be normal. I hate the word 'visitation' and will never use it. We live and function as a family, and that is exactly what I tell the boys. The only difference is that we do it a little less than other people do. The smartest decision I ever made was to encourage my sons to get permission for their friends to join us on any weekend they were available. I reasoned that a big part of everyday life for kids involves playing with their friends. I could not think of anything more normal than that.

The results have been far beyond my expectations. On any given weekend, my home is filled with the sights and sounds of four or more rambunctious little boys.[2] The roar of laughter filling the house is very cathartic. Having them around makes me forget just how much things have changed. Slowly but surely, we are finding our way.

---

[2] The two young men that I pay homage to at the beginning of this book were regular weekend warriors at our home. I had the great pleasure of watching them grow into fine young men. They became a regular part of my 'family of men' and I loved them both very much. I think of them often, and sometimes struggle to accept the fact that they are no longer with us.

The Incident

I wake in the fetal position; my arms wrapped tightly around my core. I am cold, and my body is shaking. All of my bedding lies in a tangled heap at the foot of my bed. My T-shirt is soaked and clings tightly to my body. Both the mattress and fitted sheet are damp. There is an unpleasant odor hanging in the air, a mixture of musk and stale sweat. This is the third time in less than two weeks that I've found myself in this situation.

I strip the bed and make my way downstairs to the laundry room. With a little effort, I manage to cram the entire lot into the washing machine. I set the dial for the heavy cycle and head back upstairs to shower.

I have just reached the top of the landing when the first wave descends upon me like a foreboding premonition. Within seconds, I am consumed with the kind of sadness that evokes a deep sense of loss. My face is flush, and I can feel my body temperature rapidly rising. In an instant, I am sweating profusely.

I race to the bathroom in search of a towel. The rate of perspiration is constant. It pools at my feet and rolls past my toes before collecting along the grout line. When the second wave hits, it is much stronger. Every muscle in my body tightens as if preparing for a physical assault. I am overcome with feelings of incredible loss and a sense of deep sorrow. They are the sort of emotions that are born from horrific tragedy. The whole thing feels like an out-of-body experience. I have absolutely no control over what is happening to me, and I struggle to make sense of it all.

The sweat running down my face tastes salty and stings as it floods the wells of my eyes. I reach for the shower door and turn the cold water on full. Taking a deep breath, I step into the frigid onslaught. The anticipated shock of cold water is neutralized by the extreme heat radiating from my body. I look up and rinse my eyes before exposing the rest of my body to the cooling effect of the spray.

Suddenly, I feel light-headed and wonder if the rapid loss of fluids is causing me to dehydrate. As a precaution, I lean my head back, open my mouth wide, and drink deeply. As my body temperature slowly returns to normal, the sweating spell begins to ebb. Adjusting the water temperature to lukewarm, I scrub my body clean. I try to concentrate on the task, but my mind is racing. What just happened here? None of this makes any sense.

Stepping out of the shower, I grab a towel and head for my bedroom. I am just about to pull jeans from a dresser drawer when the last and most powerful wave takes hold. It is overwhelming and consumes every part of my being. My lungs contract and my entire sensory system shifts into overdrive. Wave after wave of grief bombards me. The despair is so deep and so constant that tears rush down my face. In seconds, I am weeping uncontrollably.

I am lost in a deep black hole of sorrow. I cannot breathe, and when I do, my lungs hurt. Just when I think it's about to end, the pattern begins all over again. Two hours later, I am physically spent. Even though my tear ducts have run dry, the sobbing continues. I fall to my knees and rest my head on the barren mattress. Sleep comes quickly, and with it, relief from my nightmare.

When I wake, the room is dark, the air cool and clean. As I scan each wall, my eyes are drawn to the illuminated digits radiating from the alarm clock. The numbers are clearly visible, but they make no sense. 8:08 PM. How can that possibly be?

Using the bed for support, I pull myself up and make my way to the window. The stars shine bright, and the streetlights illuminate the ground below. A quick survey of the front yard reveals my unkempt lawn, a sober reminder of a day that somehow simply disappeared.

It seems impossible to believe, but I slept for nearly eleven hours. I struggle to find some rational explanation for what took place. It's like my entire system short-circuited and shut itself down. I reflect on the many changes that have taken place in my life over the past two years. Is this what a nervous breakdown feels like? I have no idea, but the experience has left me unsettled. The night sweats I can handle, but this is an entirely different matter.

Surprisingly, I feel fantastic and charged with energy. I doubt I will sleep much tonight, so I contemplate my list of inside chores. I look down once more at my poor lawn and shake my head. Despite the bizarre events of the day, my mood is surprisingly upbeat. I even manage to make myself laugh out loud. In my mind, I am picturing a souped-up ride-on lawn mower, fitted with a highly sophisticated noise-canceling muffler and a pair of night vision goggles. If only.

The Diagnosis

The remainder of the week is surprisingly uneventful and I quickly slip back into my rigorous routine.

This year the company has decided that all department heads should receive a thorough physical as part of an overall wellness program for senior management. All of the appointments were scheduled weeks ago. Mine is to take place at a private clinic in downtown Vancouver.

Over the years, my weight has fluctuated, and I go between struggling to stay in decent shape, to buckling down and really taking care of myself. This year I have taken full advantage of our office gym and have managed to lose a few extra pounds. I am in the best shape I've been in nearly a decade.

Since the divorce, I have gone without a family doctor. This will be a timely opportunity to make sure that everything is okay. As a private clinic, this facility caters primarily to professional athletes and looks more like a high-tech gym than a medical office.

I am waiting for my results and looking at a brochure on common sports injuries when a tall man in his mid-forties enters the examining room. He introduces himself, and we sit down to review my numbers. It appears the workouts are paying off, as my results are good. I will never be thin, but at least by sticking to my regular workouts, I am headed in the right direction. We are nearing the end of our session when he asks me if there is anything else I would like to discuss. He has been easy to talk to and given that I am without a family doctor; I decide to share the events of last Monday with him. He sits quietly without interruption. I avoid eye contact until I near the end. When I look up, I catch a look in his eyes that betrays his concern.

He smiles and asks me to describe the times I feel pressured, and the things in my life that cause me the most stress. I share with him the challenges I face balancing my business and family life. We talk about the divorce and my role as a single dad. I describe my job in detail, and when I am done, I ask him if he thinks I've experienced some sort of nervous breakdown. Rather than give me an answer, he hedges and suggests that it could be a number of different things. He recommends that I see a good friend of his who deals with various types of emotional issues.

Emotional issues? What does he mean by that? He can see that I am hesitant and assures me that the cause is likely nothing more that excess stress. He asks me to wait while he makes a call to see when I can get in.

A few minutes later, he returns and hands me a card with the name and address of the doctor I am to see. Standing outside the facility, I take a moment to review the information. It is the field of medicine that gets my full attention. He is a doctor of psychiatry. A psychiatrist? Why am I seeing a psychiatrist? I am tempted to toss the card in the trash, but instead, I place it in my wallet and head back to the office.

The appointment is scheduled for three days from today. I will have to do some major juggling and move a number of things on my calendar to make it work. Once again, I am tempted to forget the whole thing, but then I remember the look of concern on the doctor's face. The fact that he has managed to get me in so quickly suggests a sense of urgency.

***

The psychiatrist's office is located in a large complex on Broadway in Vancouver. Traffic is light this morning, and I arrive a full half-hour ahead of my appointment. I feel anxious and concentrate on taking deep breaths. I turn on the radio, but I am too agitated to sit in the car. Instead, I step out and take in some fresh air before heading into the building.

The lobby is enormous and contains a long registry of names. When I finally locate the doctor's name, I notice that there is no reference to his field. I am relieved. The last thing I want is for anyone else to know why I am here, which coincidentally turns out to be his very first question.

"So, Don, why are you here?"

The man sitting in front of me is probably in his mid to late sixties. He has a ruddy completion and unkempt hair that would have been a bright copper in his younger days. Despite being a large man, there is nothing intimidating about him. Instead, he exudes a confidence that is both reassuring and calming. The question catches me off guard, and I say, "Why am I here?"

"Yes, I assume that something has happened that is causing you some concern."

It dawns on me that the exchange between the two doctors has been limited. It is up to me to fill in the blanks, and so I begin by describing the episodes where I am drenched in sweat, and then progress to the events that occurred two Mondays ago.

"Has anything happened since then?" he asks.

I nod. "Another heavy sweating spell. This time, it occurred at work in the middle of the day. I took a quick cold shower, and it seemed to do the trick."

"All right. I want you to think back and tell me about the other times when you seemed to have been overwhelmed by emotion."

I tell him I'm not sure what he means.

"For instance, is this the first time you have felt such overpowering grief?"

It isn't. I describe the service for my grandmother, from whom I had been estranged from for nearly a decade. In my youth, she had been a huge influence in my life. I was able to reconcile with her on her deathbed, but when I was delivering her eulogy, I became overwhelmed. Despite the fact that the feelings were similar, there was one significant difference. At the service, I was grieving for my grandmother and a lost relationship, and so I felt deep sadness. In this case, there was absolutely no reason for my emotions. My family and friends were all fine, and to the best of my knowledge, nothing bad had happened to anyone I knew. The feelings I experienced, on the other hand, were very real.

The next hour and a half hour is taken up with a discussion about my family history and my childhood, leading to the present. His pattern is to ask a question, sit back and listen, and then write feverishly before asking another. He is a hard man to read, and I am having trouble deciding whether he thinks this is something serious.

Before I have a chance to ask, he suggests we schedule a second appointment and requests that I purchase a personal journal. He would like me to begin to write any physical or emotional variances that I would consider out of the norm. He then stands to signal our time is up and reminds me to bring my journal to our next session.

We will end up meeting several times in the coming weeks. The night sweats continue but are less frequent. When we meet next, I ask him if I should be taking anything. He recommends that I wait and adds that night sweats are often symptoms of something else.

To begin our third session, he focuses on comments in my journal that cover the past two days. He asks about what I describe as a super-human burst of energy. I tell him it is euphoric in nature, a natural high, and it makes me feel almost invincible. I note that for the past two nights I have slept less than two hours and yet I wake feeling completely rested and energized.

"I notice something different in your mannerisms today," he says. "Your voice is strong, and your answers are clear and concise. For the first time, you appear completely relaxed. How often do these periods of euphoria last?"

I have been looking forward to today's session. I want the doctor to see that there is nothing wrong with me. I am strong and lucid. I am sharp and capable. I'm also optimistic that whatever has plagued me is over.

"To tell you the truth, the only time I am really aware of them is when I don't require much sleep. I have definitely experienced them before, and they are incredibly exhilarating."

"Do you consider yourself to be someone with a good memory?"

"Considering how many times I lose my keys and don't seem to have a clue where I left them, I would have to say no to that. It's funny though, when I am doing a speech, I can put five words on an index card and do twenty to thirty minutes, so I guess it sort of depends."

"Do you know any poems by heart?"

This seems like an odd question, and I am about to say no when I remember that back in high school I had to memorize a poem for my Spanish class. The purpose was to grade my enunciation, but that was nearly twenty years ago. I share this with him.

"I want you to recite it for me."

"Right now?"

"Please."

Without hesitation, I begin.

"Cancion del jinete."

Córdoba,
Lejana y sola.
Jaca negra, luna grande,
y aceitunas en mi alforja,
Aunque sepa los caminos,
yo nunca llegaré a Córdoba.

He raises his hand to indicate that I may stop. I tell him I'm surprised that it has come so easily. He does not seem surprised at all. By coincidence, he spent two years doing research in Mexico City and speaks the language fluently. He tells me that my enunciation is incredibly good. He goes on to say that remembering the words is one thing, but recalling the correct pronunciation is impressive, especially after twenty years.

"How often do you practice your Spanish?"

"Not at all," I confess.

"Now that's a pity. You really should take it up again. You're a natural."

As the session ends, I am incredibly upbeat. I'm ready to declare myself cured when he asks me if we can change the day for our next session. I say no problem, but what I really want to say is, aren't we done?

We will continue for several more weeks, and it will not be until our seventh session that he feels comfortable with his diagnosis.

***

During my time as the head of the training department, I would often do speeches on behalf of the corporation on a variety of topics. In 1990, McDonald's Canada played a major role in opening our first restaurant in the Soviet Union. This was a significant accomplishment. While many prominent North American brands were being sold in the USSR, no western company was actually operating there. With the Cold War still very much in play, it was left up to diplomatic negotiations, and a great deal of patience exercised by the Canadian company, to finally ink the deal.

I was doing a presentation to a large human resources group in Winnipeg, Manitoba. My speech was to be on McDonald's entry into the Soviet Union. Fortunately, I was able to get my hands on the first McDonald's commercials produced in Russian for the Soviet market.

Any speaker will tell you that a big part of a successful presentation is the material you bring, and that day I had the mother lode. By sheer coincidence, there happened to be a headhunter in the audience who was seeking a keynote speaker for a major US convention in Southern California the following year. I was offered the job, but being a corporate employee, I was not permitted to receive any personal compensation. Instead, I requested that the entire fee be donated to Ronald McDonald's Children's Charities of Canada.

By the time the event took place, I had been promoted to operations manager for the city of Vancouver. The speech would take place a few days before my seventh session with the psychiatrist.

***

Anaheim California, February 10, 1992

It's just past three in the afternoon when I get the first sensation that something is about to happen. It is less intense than previous occasions but strong enough to cause me concern. I stand up and begin to pace the room. I am sweating, but the culprit, this time, is panic rather than any change in my body temperature. The second wave is much stronger. An overwhelming sense of grief takes hold, and the first waves of tears begin to stream down my face.

I strip off all of my clothes and make a beeline for the bathroom. Turning the tap to cold, I step into the spray. This time, the shock to my system is more than I can bear and I am forced to adjust the water temperature. Breathing deeply, I lean my head against the cold porcelain tile and sob uncontrollably.

It's hard for me to explain what these episodes are really like. In my descriptions, you will note that I do not use the word depressed. The reason is simple: In my case, I am not depressed. What I feel is a great sense of sadness, the kind of sorrow that comes with deep personal loss and tragedy. Right now, it is overwhelming and very, very real.

The shower is refreshing, but the feelings remain strong and present. I managed to stop the tears long enough to contact the woman who has been my liaison with the company. I explain that I am not feeling well and to ensure that I will be ready for tomorrow morning, I must decline the invitation to dinner. She is professional and says she understands, but I can tell that she's disappointed.

***

I consider it a great privilege to stand before an audience and deliver an entertaining performance. I have worked many long hours getting ready for this keynote address. This will be my moment, and I know the caliber of presentation that I am capable of delivering. I will not have it taken away from me.

I practice long into the evening hours, forcing myself to work through the utter sense of despair. When I finally lay down, I am physically spent. Despite my exhaustion, sleep eludes me for most of the night. I wake before the alarm clock and turn towards the sound of rain tapping on my window. Black clouds darken the morning sky and mirror the dark emotions that blanket my mind.

In the early morning light, I contemplate my options. Any thoughts of bowing out are quickly dispelled. I am determined that these people will get an entertaining presentation with boundless energy. I must find a way to make that happen. I think of the old Hollywood cliché, 'the show must go on.' I have no idea if I can pull it off, but I have made up my mind that if I don't, I will go down fighting. I begin to run through the opening in my mind as

I prepare to take a long hot shower. Finally, I make it down to the conference hall.

I open my presentation with a Russian television commercial followed by a humorous anecdote that I know is a surefire winner. The first roar of laughter is the boost that I need, and I'm on my way. Everything is going remarkably well until I come to a small bit designed to poke harmless fun at the CEO. The problem is that I can't recall his name, first or last. When the moment comes when his name becomes critical to delivering the punch line, I hesitate. My only hope to salvage this mess is to point my finger at him and say, "You know, what's his name over there."

Unfortunately, it bombs. Instead of laughter, there is complete silence, and it quickly dawns on me that everyone knows I have forgotten his name. A cardinal rule of public speaking is that when something goes wrong you pause, gather your thoughts, take a deep breath, and carry on. Instead, I resort to a total rookie move and go for a cheap laugh at the expense of the CEO. The line went something like this. "You know what they say, great men are born to do great things and are long remembered for their greatness," pause for effect, "and then there's what's his name." The roar of laughter breaks the uncomfortable silence, but I immediately regret it the moment it is out of my mouth. Even though I am working under incredibly challenging circumstances, there's no excuse for what I did.

You never make fun of those who brought you to the dance. It was unprofessional, and I know it. The look on his face confirms my regret. I manage to recover with twenty more minutes of solid material culminating in a standing ovation.

When we break for lunch, the CEO approaches me. As soon as I see him walking toward me, I instantly remember his name. Too little, too late. We shake hands, and he guides me away from the crowd. Before he can speak, I try to explain the circumstance around my indiscretion and offer my sincere apology for the cheap shot. I acknowledge that it was completely unprofessional and in poor taste. The expression on his face suggests that my apology has fallen short of the mark. It's clear in his mind that the joke crossed the line. There is no doubt that if I were one of his employees, this would be my last day.

"I have a good mind not to pay your fee," he says.

I understand how he feels, and I remain calm when I reply.

"Then it is a good thing that I'm not collecting a fee today. I'd like to remind you that your money is going to a very worthy charity. Now if you would like me to call them and explain why they will not be receiving your generous donation, then I will be happy to do that on your behalf."

I may be guilty of a major faux pas, but there is no way that the charity is going to suffer for my indiscretion.

His eyes lock onto mine for several seconds. I am uncertain whether he is trying to determine if I this is a bluff or not. The standoff abruptly ends, and he simply turns and walks away. I see him approach a young lady, and the two of them look my way. A moment later, she approaches and hands me a check made out in the full amount to RMCC. I thank her and quickly show myself out.

***

I had one personal request when we were putting the contract together. After my presentation was over, I wanted to be taken to Disneyland. I was looking forward to capping off what I believed would be a triumphant speech with an afternoon spent at 'the happiest place on earth.'

They fulfill their end of the bargain, and soon I find myself surrounded by a host of characters that I grew up watching on television. Unfortunately, even a combination of the Magic Kingdom and a return of the warm California sunshine cannot lift me out of my darkness.

Still, as I reflect on the day, I am enormously proud of myself. I have never faced such adversity, and despite the one unfortunate misstep, I have somehow managed to pull the whole thing off. As the sound of children's laughter fills the air, I sit on a bench next to the Matterhorn and make notes in my journal.

Two days later, I am back in Vancouver and ready to begin my seventh session. I am looking forward to sharing my Anaheim experience with this man who has become my most trusted ally. Even though I am extremely proud of what I was able to accomplish, I can no longer deny the fact that something is seriously wrong. When I look up he is staring out the window; his thoughts a million miles away. Suddenly he stands and gently places his hand upon my shoulder. As he looks into my eyes, my heart begins to race. In this critical moment I have no idea what he is about to say, but somehow I know it is going to change my life.

"Don, I want to begin by saying that I think it is highly unlikely that this all began a few weeks ago. I believe that there have been signs for a long time that may not have been quite as acute as what you are now experiencing. I suspect that this may have even contributed to some of your marital problems.

"Taking into account everything you have shared with me over these many weeks, it is my professional opinion that you have bipolar disorder. It results from a chemical imbalance that short-circuits the part of the brain that regulates moods and emotions. Some people have infrequent episodes and can go weeks, months, and even years without a single serious incident while other people experience more frequent episodes that are far more severe. Yours is one of the most aggressive cases that I have ever personally come across. We refer to the most extreme cases as rapid-cycle bipolar disorder."

I am stunned and can barely breathe.

"Are you telling me that I am mentally ill?"

"I am saying that there are many different types of mental disorders, and this happens to be one of them. There are medications that can help you manage your life, but you need to understand that they are not a cure."

As the session ends, I feel numb. He asks me if there is anyone he can call who could come pick me up. I assure him that I am capable of driving myself home. As I pull into my driveway, my phone rings. It's my secretary, wondering where I am. At first, I'm confused by her question until I remember that I have a full slate of work ahead of me today. I try to remain calm as I tell her that an emergency has come up and that I will have to take the rest of the day off. I ask her to make my apologies and see if she can reschedule my meetings and appointments.

I place my head on the steering wheel and for the first time since the diagnosis, I allow myself to cry. This time, the tears are not caused by some freakish imbalance but by genuine sadness. I am only thirty-seven years old and for the first time in my life, I feel completely helpless. What am I going to do?

I feel nothing but shame. I know that none of this is my fault, but it does nothing to change the way I feel. I am deeply ashamed. How could I let this happen? I am a bright person. I am also articulate and clear-minded. The doctor has to be wrong. This is a nightmare, a total nightmare. The only problem is; I am not dreaming.

Mental illness is a topic that tends to make everyone feel a little uncomfortable. Before my diagnosis, I had never even heard of bipolar disorder. We have a tendency when it comes to mental illnesses to lump them all together and base our opinions on behaviors associated with some of the most serious ones such as schizophrenia, autism, and paranoia.

We see mentally ill people as unstable, dysfunctional, and unpredictable. Many of us would have a hard time imagining a mentally ill person capable of being an effective leader. It's just a reality of the stigma that is often attached to the disease. I think the biggest personal lesson I learned from my own experience is that leadership comes in all shapes and sizes. For me, it was all about investing in people who would play an important part in helping me to build a successful business. Some of the most powerful and effective leaders in the world are soft spoken and humble people. Leadership is what you make it. While I would never wish my illness on my worst enemy, I learned a long time ago that only I can choose to see it as a handicap.

***

The upper management of our company is predominantly a collection of alpha males. We have some talented women making a mark for themselves, but for now, this is still very much a boy's club. It is a highly competitive environment where any sign of weakness is viewed by others as an opportunity. It might sound harsh, but it is all part of the toughness, both mental and physical, that is required to be successful when competing for the top positions in any large organization. The more I think about the environment I work in, the more convinced I am that no one must ever know. I don't know what I am going to do. I am due back to work tomorrow, and I am scared to death that something will happen that will expose the truth.

I wrestle with my dilemma all night. Sleep will not come, so I sit in the kitchen and rest my head in my hands. I have a second sabbatical coming up in the new year that would entitle me to just over three months off when combined with my regular holidays. At first, the idea sounds appealing, but then I realize there are two significant problems. The first is that when I return, I will still have the disease. Hopefully, I will have had some success with the drugs, and perhaps I will have found other ways to minimize the effects, but I will still have to return to the rigors of my job. The bigger problem is that I will have to explain why I am requesting the time off on such short notice. Although I have the highest regard for the men who run our company, I am not ready to go that far. I am convinced that the truth will leak out, and I will never be taken seriously again.

The shame that overwhelms me, and the genuine fear of others knowing, forces me to embrace a far more drastic decision. In the morning, I will resign and start my life all over again.

***

To say that there is a buzz flying around the office would be an understatement. My resignation takes everyone by surprise, and there is great speculation about the reason. In my letter, I state that I have always loved to teach, which is true, and I have decided that before I get too old, I would like to complete my education and earn my teaching degree.

I suspect that I will be called into a meeting, and it occurs on Tuesday afternoon. At the table are Ken Bathurst, head of human resources and a real quality guy. Next to him is my direct boss, Arnie Nelson, the company vice president and an extraordinary man whom I fully respect. The final member of the group is Ron Marcoux, the executive vice president whose praises I have already sung but bear repeating. He has been at the helm of the company for all the years that I have worked there. I have nothing but the highest regard for this man.

They grill me extensively but to no avail. I can tell that they're not buying my reason for leaving, but I hold firm. This has come completely out of nowhere and makes no sense to any of them. It takes every fiber in my body to remain calm. The truth is, I have absolutely no idea what I am going to do, but I cannot let on that I am terrified. I apologize for the short notice. I know that our Christmas party will occur in just a few days. For our company, this is not only the annual office and managers' party but also the time when all the strategic promotions in the company are announced.

I know that I've left them little time to choose my successor, but I also know that this is a company way ahead of its time when it comes to succession planning. There is always a Plan B waiting in the wings, and whatever it is, it's about to be put into play. The meeting ends cordially with handshakes and best wishes all around.

I do not attend the Christmas party. It would be the perfect opportunity to say goodbye to everyone, but I'm not sure I would be able to hold it together. I also know I'd be asked a thousand questions I have no intention of answering. My last day will be the fifteenth of December, and then I'll take my remaining holidays.

When a high-profile job such as this one changes hands, there is really no transitional period. The new person is anxious to get started and will have their own agenda. They are more than capable of taking over, and so they quietly wait in the wings.

When I walk out of the office on my last day, I am totally convinced that I will never set foot in this building again. As it turns out, that won't be true. My good friend fate is about to intervene for the second time in this story. It will not happen for several months, but when it does, it will occur in a most unusual way.

***

It was a tough Christmas. I have just given up the security of a job that has been my bread and butter for more than two decades. The boys are to spend the better part of the holidays with me, and I pray that I will not suffer a major episode. Fortunately, I am spared, and do my best to make it an enjoyable time for everyone.

I put on a brave face when I tell my family that I am leaving McDonald's. Becoming a teacher was something I seriously considered when I was much younger. This has become far more than a convenient excuse for my departure. It's a real opportunity for a brand new start, away from the people who know me best. I need to research my options for acquiring my degree, but first I must begin my treatment.

During my final visit to see my psychiatrist, I thank him for the way he took me through the process. I can tell that he is genuinely concerned about my welfare. I elect not to tell him that I've left my job but agree to treatment providing it is not local. I am paranoid about any paper trail. It may sound irrational, but it's the only way I will do it.

He tells me that he has a colleague in Washington State whom he will ask to take my case. It happens that there is an upcoming session at a facility just outside Seattle for people dealing with the disorder. I have no idea what to expect, but I agree to attend. He strongly suggests that I have members of my family participate in the meeting since it will be informative for my support team. I thank him again, and we hug.

Support team? I'm just beginning to come to terms with what I'm dealing with myself, so I opt to attend the session on my own.

We have just finished the education/informational side of the workshop when we are asked to form smaller groups and spread out in the room. In my group is a mother with her daughter who has just been diagnosed. She is only eighteen years old. Next to them sits a man in his early forties, who has also just received his diagnosis. He is joined by his wife, their young daughter, and their teenage son. We are asked to share our personal experiences, but when it comes around to the other fellow's turn to speak, he begins to weep instead. He looks weathered and broken. As he struggles to gain control, I see his son rise and wrap his arms around his father. With the strength in his voice of someone far beyond his years he says, "Don't worry, Dad, everything is going to be just fine. I am going to take care of you from now on."

As I look at his wife with tears flowing down her face, I realize their lives have been forever changed. I am feeling so bad for this man that I nearly forget that I am in the same predicament. As I witness the despair that surrounds me, I make an important decision. I will not do this to my family. I may have failed at marriage, and I may have just quit the only job I have ever known, but there's no way I will give up my role as protector of my sons.

They are just ten and eleven years old, and it's my job to be their strength. It was never meant to be the other way round. I look again into the eyes of these women who cannot help but feel pity for their loved ones. I realize that for these families, the traditional dynamic will never be the same. When I think of my family, of my mother and father in particular, and how much they've already sacrificed for me, I will not burden them with this. They are worriers by nature, and this will have a drastic impact on the quality of their lives.

Through time and circumstance, I have become the dominant strength in our family. I am the go-to guy, the one who can be counted on for anything. I will not allow that to change; I won't let it happen.

This could have been the end of the Quadrant Leadership story were it not for a chance encounter that would mark my return to the company I thought was lost to me forever.

***

A popular feature of sit-down restaurants in the early nineties in Canada is decadent salad bars. One of these restaurants is located in the city of Surrey and is a particular favorite of my boys. The time of year is now early March. We have just been seated when I feel a tap on my shoulder. It is Ron Marcoux. He and his wife Gayle are sitting across the room. He waits for the boys to head up to the salad bar before speaking. He begins by asking how I am doing, and I give him the perfunctory all's well. What he is to say next will change the course of events one more time.

"I know your reasons for leaving were personal, and I respect that, but I thought after all of these years, we could be truthful with one another. You said that becoming a teacher was why you left, but I don't buy it. I think you owe me the truth."

He can see that the boys are about to rejoin me at the table. I have just a few seconds to reply. In that moment, I make the decision to trust this man who has been such an important influence in my life.

"You're right, Ron; there is more to the story. If you are going to be around the office on Monday, I will drop by and share it with you."

"I appreciate that. How about ten o'clock?"

"That sounds fine. I'll see you then."

Ron was right, I did owe him a better explanation. He had been a great supporter of my place in the company. At one point, he even appointed me a guest advisor to join him at the board meetings held in Toronto. On the plane ride down, he would talk frankly about things that most people were never privy to hear. I used to think that he was testing my ability to hold confidence, which I always did. I never discussed any of our conversations with anyone else.

We meet on Monday morning, and I tell him the entire story. When I finish he says, "Is that all? Is that the reason you walked away from your career?"

I'm not certain he grasps the seriousness of my illness, and I am about to say so when he continues.

"You are not the first, nor will you be the last guy to have to deal with these types of issues."

I sense that he has no intention of being more specific, so I decide to take him at his word.

"When can you start?" he asks.

"You mean you want me to come back?

"Of course I want you back. I will have to meet with Arnie to go over the details, but one of us will get back to you within a day."

The only request I make is that only he, Arnie, and Ken are to know the truth. He gives me his word that my confidence will be kept. I leave both elated and terrified. I feel so genuinely grateful to be valued like this, but I am unsure how the pressures of the job will affect my illness.

I assume I will start with a demotion since there are no department head jobs available, but instead, I am returned to my full salary and put on special projects. My service record is restored, and my time away is recorded as my second sabbatical. Just before the hectic summer months arrive, a position opens up, and I am once again an operations manager.

Over the course of the next two years, I will perform my duties to the very best of my ability. By the summer of 1993, the challenges of my illness and the rigors of the job are beginning to place a significant toll on my health once more.

I sit down with Arnie to discuss my future and to make a request. I asked that he and Ron consider giving me an opportunity to become an owner/operator. By implementing Quadrant Leadership, I believe that I will be able to create the breathing room I need to manage my illness.

He assures me that he will discuss it with Ron and let me know when they have made their decision.

I will not hear back for several months. On a warm autumn afternoon, I receive the news that I have been longing to hear. In the new year, I will become an owner/operator with my own restaurant right here in the city of Vancouver.

***

Fate was to intervene, not once but twice at a critical time in my life. What were the odds that a pre-scheduled routine physical would take place just days after my first episode, or that a simple dinner out with my sons would lead to a chance encounter with Ron Marcoux?

There is no doubt in my mind that had there been no bipolar disorder; there would have been no Quadrant Leadership. From personal tragedy came a remarkable discovery. The results that my company was able to achieve even as I struggled to deal with my new reality are what gives Quadrant Leadership its credibility. "The more people know, the more they are capable of contributing" is so much more than a catchy slogan. It is the payback that comes from the time invested in the model. By significantly improving the performance of my employees, I drastically improved my odds for success. What constantly amazed me was just how much more my employees were capable of when given the opportunity to exercise their true potential.

There is no doubt in my mind that any boss who is prepared to commit to this extraordinary approach to leadership, and fully embrace the Quadrant Leadership Model, will achieve results far beyond their wildest expectations.

Before I leave my personal story behind and move on to the nuts and bolts of Quadrant Leadership, there is one more group of people I would like to recognize. They played a critical role in my success, and I will forever be in their debt. My psychiatrist was right when he said that I would need a solid support team. For me, that group has always been my extraordinary friends. I am blessed with many rich and enduring friendships. I consider myself to be a lucky man. My philosophy is that you can never have too many friends, and I will forever be grateful for their unwavering support. The greatest gift they ever gave me was never to change the way they saw me. I could not ask for more.

Canción del jinete

Córdoba.
Lejana y sola.

Jaca negra, luna grande,
y aceitunas en mi alforja.
Aunque sepa los caminos,
yo nuca llegaré a Córdoba.

Por el llano, por el viento,
jaca negra, luna roja.
La muerte me está mirando
desde las torres de Córdoba.

¡Ay que camino tan largo!
¡Ay mi jaca valerosa!
¡Ay que la muerte me espera,
antes de llegar a Córdoba!

Córdoba.
Lejana y sola.

-Federico Garcia Lorca

Horeman's Song

Cordoba.
Distant and alone.

A black nag, the giant moon,
and olives in my saddle bag.
Even if I know the way,
I never will reach Cordoba.

Over the plain, through the wind,
A black nag, the bloody moon.
The Reaper is watching me
From the tall towers of Cordoba.

Oh, such a long road!
Oh, my valiant nag!
Oh, the Reaper awaits me
before I ever reach Cordoba!

Cordoba.
Distant and alone.

- Translation, Charles W. Johnson

Part Three

Transitioning to Quadrant Leadership

Introducing the Quadrant Leadership Model	78
Optimizing Pareto's Law	82
Preparing to Transition	86
The Transition Journal	88
Creating Free and Flexible Time	92
Integrating Your Core Team into Quadrant Leadership	101
The Main Event	106

A good education can prepare a person for life.
A good business education can set them for life.

Introducing the Quadrant Leadership Model

At the core of our public education system is the principle of progressive development where knowledge is layered, and in some cases more complex concepts and ideas are given time to comprehend fully.

Traditionally in the workplace, we take an entirely different approach to employee development. Most jobs are front-loaded, with the majority of dedicated training taking place in the first few weeks of employment, or when an employee is transitioning into a new job. Additional training is usually reactive in nature, triggered by the specific needs of the company.

Employees are largely expected to carry out their duties to the best of their ability with on the job experience often becoming their primary teacher. We look for self-starters who exercise natural leadership abilities to target for future development while often failing to recognize the potential of employees who simply do not stand out from the crowd.

With Quadrant Leadership, we take an entirely different approach to preparing our employees for the role they will play in our business by fully embracing the principle of progressive development. To guide us through the process, we use a tool called the Quadrant Leadership Model. The model acts as both a roadmap and a platform for all employee development. Given the incredible importance of this tool, let's take a closer look at it now.

Each of the four quadrants in the model approaches employee development from an entirely different perspective. Specific needs will dictate which quadrant or quadrants will be best suited to accomplish the task at hand. The primary objective of every quadrant is to build upon the employee's knowledge base.

Quadrant Leadership takes full advantage of information-sharing techniques and explores subject matter not typically addressed in traditional training models. Long before we ever attempt to put into practice any actionable behavior associated with a new concept or principle, we ensure that the employee has all of the knowledge and tools they need to be successful.

My background in employee development certainly gave me a leg up when it came to bringing the model to life, but I want to assure you that any boss can be as successful as I was. With today's technology, you need only look to the Internet to discover a wealth of material that will serve as a great employee development resource for your company.

Let's take a quick look at the primary objective of each of the four quadrants. Later in the book, we will get into each one in far more detail.

The first quadrant is called **The Trainer/Expert**. Here the focus is on acquiring the skills and technical knowledge necessary for employees to carry out the fundamentals of their job description at a competent level. The majority of employee training that takes place in this quadrant is completed by your subject matter experts. Your personal involvement in the first quadrant will depend entirely on the nature of your business and the number of employees in your company.

The Teacher/Philosopher quadrant is the quadrant of reciprocal dialogue where free-thinking is encouraged to ensure that your employees are able to grasp less tangible concepts and principles that play a vital role in their ability to perform to their full potential. Taking a philosophical approach to learning triggers a deeper sense of understanding and allows the employee to explore the rationale behind why and how things are done a certain way, or to a certain standard. This kind of dialogue is critical to your employee's ability to gain a deeper appreciation for the contributions they will be expected to make to your company.

The third quadrant in the model is called **The Observer/Coach**. To reap the benefits of this quadrant, you must have a clear understanding of the difference between coaching and teaching. Effective coaching techniques take time to master and do not come naturally to most people. When executed properly they challenge the employee's ability to resolve issues and make effective decisions based solely on their own resources.

The last quadrant in the model is **The Mentor/Advisor**. This quadrant explores the critical role that mentorship can play in breaking down barriers that are inhibiting an employee's ability to grow. While there is a great deal that can be accomplished in this quadrant, there are specific parameters that must be in place before it can ever be enacted.

The more familiar you are with the model, the easier it becomes to implement. There is no such thing as a right or wrong way to put it into practice. In most cases, common sense and logic will dictate which quadrant will be best suited to address a particular development opportunity. For brand new or existing employees who are taking on new job responsibilities, their development tends to follow a natural progression through the first three quadrants. Combined, these quadrants represent one complete cycle of development. This is a major achievement that is validated through the certification process.

Preparation time for any given session will depend entirely on your own level of experience and expertise, and the nature of the situation that you are dealing with. Take heart in knowing that the more sessions you conduct, the less preparation time you will require. Never underestimate what you already bring to the table, but also look for new sources of material that will provide your employees with the kind of insight that will capitalize on their true potential.

The Quadrant Leadership Model was designed solely for employee development and never intended to be used to critique or inspect employee performance. The whole objective of Quadrant Leadership is to build an extraordinary army of brand builders capable of taking your company to a whole new level.

Optimizing Pareto's Law

Pareto's law explores the unique relationship between cause and effect. Based on the research of Italian economist Vilfredo Pareto it suggests that some of the things we do for our business contribute far more to our success than others. It is more commonly referred to as the 80/20 rule. Pareto discovered that in many cases, eighty percent of the effects, or the results you are hoping to achieve, can be attributed to just twenty percent of the causes. The key is to identify the primary activities that make up that twenty percent. It makes no difference whether you call them principles, values, objectives, initiatives, activities, or beliefs, the bottom line is that these are the core activities that define the essence of your brand.

When I was an operations manager, I did not have direct contact with every employee, so I had to stay focused on the message. The key to McDonald's success lies in executing the core values of the McDonald's brand, or as Ray Kroc would have said, outstanding QSC.

As an owner/operator with Quadrant Leadership at my disposal, I had a distinct advantage. I could be far more specific when determining which elements would yield the highest return based on the cause and effect equation. While running an outstanding restaurant would always be the goal, the key to my success would rest with my employees. In short, they were my twenty percent. It was obvious to me that their ability to deliver superior QSC meant that I would be optimizing the 80/20 rule.

The secret to finding success with Pareto's Law lies in two elements that are not specifically expressed in the formula. Each is critical to optimizing the cause and effect principle. Those two elements are **commitment** and **focus**.

To illustrate my point, all we need do is look at Pareto's Law in reverse. The other side of the equation suggests that a full eighty percent of the things that tend to keep us busy will contribute very little to the overall success of our business. I call these distractions **busy-work**, and they have the potential to take valuable time and resources away from the core activities that get results.

A more accurate version of Pareto's Law for a business might look like this:

$$20 \bullet 80 \bullet 80 \bullet 20$$

Expressed in words in might read: The core values and guiding principles that are the cornerstone of your brand identity will generate eighty percent of your long-term market share, providing you are prepared to commit eighty percent of your time, fully vested in executing those same brand values.

As the boss, you are continually confronted by the eighty percent of things that do little to advance your business. During the transition phase, your primary goal will be to create what we will refer to as free and flexible time. As part of that process, you will be required to take a hard look at your ability to place trust in others.

You may remember that in the Taxman Cometh, the auditor who visited my restaurant could not believe that I would turn over responsibility for conducting such an important task to my managers. What he failed to understand was that I had personally trained them in all of the administrative aspects of the business. I knew they were more than capable of taking my place and more importantly, I had other priorities where my time would be better spent. The outstanding results that followed only served to add to his total bewilderment.

The transition phase is all about creating the free and flexible time that will be needed to bring the model to life. To make that happen, many of the things that currently form part of your job description will no longer be your responsibility. This will lead to changes in the job descriptions of some of your key employees. The bottom line is that you will be wiping the slate clean, redefining not only your role in the company but also the roles of other people in current positions of authority.

Before we go any further let me say this: Quadrant Leadership is a unique and richly rewarding leadership style, but it is not for everyone. I have encountered two specific types of bosses who are unlikely to make a successful transition.

The first are those who are compelled to hold on to control of every aspect of their business. They tend to be micro-managers who are unable to let go of many of the things that would free up their time. They often have trust issues, and because they cannot turn over important tasks to others, they will never find enough time to commit fully to the implementation of the Quadrant Leadership Model.

The second type is the boss that derives no pleasure what so ever from developing people. The opportunity to share knowledge does not motivate them. They would rather hire talent than create it. They tend to be impatient, which is not a good quality for a teacher. They prefer to spend as little time as possible interacting with their employees and often hide behind closed doors. They would rather do paperwork, attend meetings, talk on the telephone, or do any one of the myriad of other activities that fall under the busy-work umbrella. They see employee development as a job that is best delegated to others.

In the next chapter on transitioning, we will tackle the whole time commitment issue. For now, think about it as time spent promoting the core values of your brand. If you say you have the best service in town, then you had better be able to prove it, day in and day out.

Much of your day deals with making countless decisions. The goal of Quadrant Leadership is to raise the expectation we have for our employees and increase the accountability level that they are required to bring to the table. One of your primary objectives is to make them far more accountable for the decisions they make on behalf of the company.

In the end, the time commitment issue will work itself out naturally. When you see what the model can do for your business, it will be all the motivation you will require. Personally, I never grew tired of the process and was constantly amazed at how much more my employees were capable of when given the opportunity to exercise their true potential.

Look to the 80/20 rule to help you determine where to use effectively your time. Every development opportunity that you take on has the potential to improve your business in some way. The key is to try to identify the opportunities where you are likely to realize the greatest return for the time invested.

Preparing to Transition

80% of My Time. Really?

For many small business owners, the idea of spending eighty percent of their time dedicated to employee development seems excessive, if not unrealistic. To achieve the kind of results that Quadrant Leadership is more than capable of delivering, you must be able to recognize the direct connection between enriched employee development and superior brand integrity. While deep discounts and strong marketing campaigns can attract customers to your business, earning the kind of loyalty that keeps them coming back requires real substance. You can not be outstanding at what you do one day and mediocre the next. A credible brand is a brand that is built on consistency. Your customers could care less what your day to day challenges are. If you want them to make a solid commitment to your business, you need to deliver on the promises of your brand each and every time they choose you over one of your competitors. Quadrant Leadership provides you with an extraordinary opportunity to free yourself from the kind of repetitive direction that does little to change future behavior. Creating a credible brand requires the commitment and the talent of many people. The more time you are able to invest in raising the performance level of your employees, the more you will come to realize just how much more they are capable of contributing.

One of the main reasons why copycats are never able to take market share away from a well run business for any sustained period of time is because they lack the kind of brand integrity that earns a customer's loyalty. There is only one sure-fire way to create long-term market share, and that is to earn it by being the best at what you do.

The Transition Journal

Before you can begin the process of creating free and flexible time, you must first have a clear idea of where your time is currently being spent. It might seem obvious to you since you live it every day, but it is not unusual to discover that our perceptions are often wrong.

To accomplish this task, we use the Transition Journal. Your goal will be to record how you currently use your time for an entire month. While the idea of keeping such a detailed journal might seem like a daunting task, it will prepare you for a smooth transition into Quadrant Leadership.

There is no need to record **time spent on customer-driven activities.** *For the purpose of this exercise, we will define them as time spent directly on the creation, design, manufacture, implementation, and/or delivery of goods and services directly to the customer.* In a perfect world, this is exactly where you should be spending the majority of your time.

It does not matter what kind of journal you use. The important thing is to record just how much of your time is spent in each of the following four categories. The information you collect here will play an important role in assessing what your next steps will be.

1. Time-Sensitive Critical Tasks.

By definition, these are administrative tasks that occur daily, weekly, or monthly that if left undone, will have an immediate and adverse effect on the business. Examples of time-sensitive critical tasks are things such as the company payroll, staff scheduling, banking, and ordering. Record only the time sensitive critical tasks that you do yourself.

2. Time Tolerant Relevant Tasks

These are tasks that are important because they are crucial to keeping the business running smoothly but do not occur within a specific deadline. They are similar to critical tasks in that failing to complete them will have an adverse effect on the business. The difference is that they are far more time tolerant. Examples vary widely depending on the industry and type of business. The bottom line is that these tasks also place demands on you and have the potential to take away from the free and flexible time you will require to invest in the model. Generic examples here will include things like dealing with maintenance and repair issues, paying bills, or implementing marketing strategies. Even something as basic as placing an office supply order would be considered a relevant task if you do it yourself. Here again, we are only looking at the tasks that currently occupy your time.

3. Busy Work

The 80/20 rule serves to remind us that it is easy to find ourselves engaged in activities that do little to make our business better. These activities can be triggered by internal and external sources.

Most of the internal busy-work that takes place in our business is reactive rather than proactive in nature. Firefighting and troubleshooting are perfect examples of busy-work. The best way to eliminate internal busy-work is to make sure the job is done right in the first place.

One of the reasons that Quadrant Leadership is so effective in eliminating internal busy-work is because of the time we invest in significantly raising job proficiency. In the second and third quadrants, our employees are introduced to a number of basic and advanced self-initiative attributes that are essential to improving job performance. With each cycle through the model, our employees are able to demonstrate their ability to contribute to the company in a far more significant way. The net result is that busy-work declines and personal accountability grows.

There are many external drivers of busy-work. As you begin to make notations in your Transition Journal, you will gain a far greater sense of just how much of your time is taken up by the wishes and demands of others.

Examples of external busy-work drivers include telephone calls, text messages, emails, and even meetings. Each has the potential to shift focus away from critical activities that build long-term market share. In a later chapter, I will address electronic communications specifically. I call this medium the godfather of busy-work because of how we have become conditioned to react to it.

Do not be fooled into thinking that just because an activity has something to do with your business that it is not busy-work. The litmus test for busy-work is very simple: If you are reacting to a situation or issue, there is a good chance that you are dealing with busy- work.

4. Employee Issues.

Any employee-related issue that hinders your business, and the time it takes to deal with these situations, should be recorded here. Examples include employees who show up late for work or fail to show up at all, as well as poor performance issues and poor people practices that require some form of conflict resolution.

Filling a shift would fall under busy-work because it is reactive in nature, but addressing the employee who created the need is an employee issue. The good news is that the action plan for these situations will be the implementation of the model itself. By choosing your under-performers as the first group of employees to go through the model, you are optimizing Pareto's Law.

Because these employees are currently contributing the least to your company, they have the potential to show the greatest improvement. Each time you are successful in turning one of these employees around, you reduce the amount of time that is taken up with employee triggered issues. Focusing your time on the causes that are likely to yield the greatest return on investment is a perfect example of the 80/20 rule in action.

Creating Free and Flexible Time

> **1. Time-Sensitive Critical Tasks**
>
> *def. - routine tasks that occur on a daily, weekly, or monthly basis that, if left undone, will have an immediate and adverse effect on the business.*

The time frame required to transition into Quadrant Leadership will depend entirely on your current situation. It has a lot to do with your existing support team. For you to change your role within the company, it will become necessary to hand over some important tasks to other members of your core team. Keep in mind that we are talking about a permanent change. Quadrant Leadership is going to demand a great deal of your time, and while these critical tasks are incredibly important to the business, your time will be required elsewhere. While you may choose to assign these tasks to specific members of your team for their personal development, the only time you should personally get involved in completing them after your transition is in an emergency situation. Turning these tasks over to other members of your team will involve creating a Critical Task Action Plan. Here is an example of what your action plan might look like.

CRITICAL TASK	PERSON RESPONSIBLE	TRAINING TIME FRAME IF APPLICABLE	TRANSITION DATE
DAILY BANKING AND BOOKKEEPING	John / Carol / Ryan	three weeks	March 15th
PURCHASING	Ryan	one month	March 26th
PAYROLL	Carol	one month	March 26th
STAFF SCHEDULE	John	one month	March 26th
ACCOUNTS RECEIVABLE	Ryan	two months	April 15th

There may be specific tasks on both your Critical and Time Tolerant action plans that involve access to financial and confidential records. For that reason, you may be reluctant to let them go. Your concern is completely valid. Unfortunately, every task that you hang on to robs you of critical time needed to implement the Quadrant Leadership Model.

The success of Quadrant Leadership relies on your willingness to place trust in others. There is no way to implement the model effectively and hang on to all of these tasks as well. You will never find enough time in a day. The support you receive from your core team, and your ability to trust key employees, is critical to your success. Let's examine trust as we define it in the model. It may help you to decide whom you will assign certain tasks to.

The first level is referred to as **untested** or **gut trust**. This occurs when two people with no prior relationship find themselves in a situation where one person must place their trust in the other. If you think about it, this happens all of the time in our everyday lives. This level of trust carries the highest degree of risk since there is no history to base our decision on, and yet people use their gut feelings to place trust in other people all of the time. In the

Quadrant Leadership Model, untested trust only comes into play at the beginning, since our goal is to build quickly a healthy and productive relationship with our employees.

The whole discussion on trust is a philosophical one that takes place in the second quadrant. Every employee is told that they have an opportunity to climb the trust ladder. Their goal is to get to the top. This is another example of the unique approach to employee development that we take in Quadrant Leadership. Employees learn that trust is a privilege that is earned. Your goal is to have every employee place value and priority on earning trust.

The second level is therefore **earned trust**. As an employee progresses in their development, we continue to give them more responsibility, which ultimately will test their ability to earn more of our trust. They learn early on that there are consequences for failing the trust test. The reality is that the ladder gets longer, and the climb harder. As each employee climbs the trust ladder, they are praised and given more opportunity to grow.

At the top of the ladder is **unconditional trust**. This level is reserved for employees with the highest integrity. They are honorable people who have earned the right to be called trustworthy. These individuals would be ideal candidates to take over any of the critical and relevant tasks identified in your action plan.

A personal example of this relates to signing authority for my company. When I was a McDonald's owner/operator, most other owners, and their spouses would be the only signing authority. No one else could write a check to pay the bills or purchase goods. I remember the day I called my accountant Jerry Miachika and told him that I was giving Mike, my restaurant manager, signing authority for the company up to $100,000. You can only imagine his reaction.

I have enormous respect for Jerry and understood his concerns, but there were two things I knew that he did not. The first was that I had no intention of spending my time on administrative tasks. I knew that it would take away from the precious time I would need to bring the Quadrant Leadership Model to life. Second, and perhaps far more important, Mike had earned my unconditional trust. I knew that he was more likely to jump off a bridge than steal one penny from me.

When someone has reached the unconditional level, it tells you a great deal about their character. Mike Trask was an excellent manager. He is a first-class individual and an honorable man, whom I was fortunate to have worked alongside the entire time that I owned my company.

I realize there are many bosses, some of whom I know personally, who cannot go there. No matter how loyal the employee has been, or how highly regarded they are, they are never permitted to rise to the level of unconditional trust.

So much of my personal success in life has come from placing trust in others. These people have earned my utmost respect. I have a line that speaks to this. "Surround yourself with experts that you truly trust, and then let them do their jobs." I live and breathe this philosophy, and it has served me well.

When I first approached my friends to ask for their support as I battled my illness, I had to trust that they would hold my confidence. These are people with great integrity that I have the highest regard for, and true to their word, they never once betrayed my trust in them. The truth is that there is always a risk when you leave something in someone else's hands. In the end, you alone can decide if you are ready to take this kind of risk.

There is no doubt that these administrative tasks are important to the business, but they can be time-consuming. I would rather be doing the things that I know will continue to grow my business than sit in an office doing paperwork.

Trust may have risk attached to it, but it is incredibly empowering. An interesting thing begins to happen when people realize that your trust in them is genuine. They make it their mission to try and never to let you down.

Each activity that currently falls on your Critical Task Action Plan takes time to complete. This is valuable time that you will require to take full advantage of the Quadrant Leadership Model. Hopefully, you have some good people that have earned your unconditional trust to carry out these tasks on your behalf. You may need to do a bit of soul-searching, but if you are successful in removing all of these things from your plate, you will have taken a major step on the road to a successful transition.

2. Time-Tolerant Relevant Tasks.

def. Tasks that are critical to the operation of your business but occur on a random basis throughout the course of the month.

These Relevant Tasks are just as important as Critical Tasks, but they can also be extremely time-consuming. During the transition phase, your goal is to continue to build upon your free and flexible time. While there is no question that these tasks are extremely important to your business, they have the potential to rob you of critical time that is vital to implementing the Quadrant Leadership Model. By creating a similar action plan for Relevant Tasks, you take the first steps to assuring that each of these jobs will be done properly by competent people. Since these tasks are less frequent and more time tolerant, the sense of urgency is not quite the same. Keep in mind that the more of these tasks you hang on to, the less time you will have for Quadrant Leadership.

In my story *The Taxman Cometh* you might remember that I did not carry a set of keys for my business, nor did I know the combination to my own safe. The poor government auditor was convinced that I was a total basket case. He could not figure out how my people knew so much when I could not even unlock the front door. Only you can decide how far you are prepared to go to free up your time. I still smile when I remember the look on that poor man's face when I told him I had no idea what the combination to the safe was.

3. Busy-work

It's important that you recognize when your time is being wasted on busy-work. While it is impossible to eliminate these activities completely, you must remain vigilant and recognize when your time, or that of your employees, is being taken up with busy-work. You will be amazed when you complete your journal just how much of your time is currently being spent on telephone calls, reading and sending emails and text messages, and attending meetings.

Each time you record one of these in your journal, ask yourself this simple question: Did the time spent on this activity support my core initiatives, or did it redirect my time elsewhere? Before you answer too quickly, think about it carefully.

A big factor will relate to the nature of your business. Any phone call, message, or sales meeting that is customer-driven is not busy-work. Anything you can do for a customer is usually a good thing. What I am talking about here is time spent on activities that have nothing to do with protecting the core values of your brand.

Some of you spend a great deal of your time in meetings. In a stand-alone chapter called *Meetings Versus Power Briefings*, I will address this in more detail. I consider the majority of meetings to be a total waste of valuable time and resources. We will explore how power briefings can be used to replace meetings and turn this form of busy-work into something that is core-driven, results orientated, and an effective use of time. You will never rid yourself of busy-work. The objective of the journal is to become aware of how you are currently spending a large percentage of your time. Many activities will appear on your busy-work list, but the following are some of the more common ones.

Examples of common busy-work activites

- **Any text message or email** that redirects your focus away from the activities that support your core objectives. Record the time it takes to read these messages and to respond to them. Do not be mislead by the fact that it has something to do with your business. If it is reactive in nature and requires your time to fix something that was not properly addressed in the first place, or avoided completely by good sound decision making, then it is busy work.

- **Phone calls.** Same as above. If it is driven by someone else's agenda or is reactive in nature, it is busy-work. Record the length of the call and any subsequent time spent addressing the nature of the call.

- **Meetings**. Many of you spend hours in meetings. I consider the majority of meetings to be one of the biggest time wasters of all. Record the time it takes to prepare for the meeting and all of the time the meeting takes you way from the core activities of your business.

- **Any element of fire fighting or trouble shooting**. This is generic to the points above, and is directed at any activity that shifts your focus. While the activity may have something to do with the business, it is usually a form of damage control rather than proactive activities that build customer counts and top line sales. All of these are considered busy-work.

- **Any time allocated to the prioities of others**, rather than the priorities of your department or business or company. These include time imposed by others in positions of authority, your parent company, or any other person who places their agenda ahead of your own.

- **Every other activity that absorbs your time but has little to do with your business.**

Let me say again, if the nature of your business involves using these communication tools to interact directly with your customers, then they are examples of core initiatives and not busy-work. Customer interaction, regardless of the form it takes, is usually a very good thing.

The key is to be diligent. Don't be fooled into thinking that because a particular phone call or message relates in some way to your business that it is an effective use of your time. If there is no measurable return for the time invested, such as cash in the register, a future order placed, or a new customer recruited, then it is likely busy-work.

It takes time to differentiate these activities, but once you do, you will see why so much time in business is reactive rather than proactive. You need to be selfish and protect not only your time but the time of those who work for you as well. Busy-work is unproductive work, no matter who is doing it.

***

There is no set timeline to complete the transition phase, but typically at the six-week mark, here is where you should be:

- Accurate assessment as to where your time is currently being spent based on the data collected in your transition journal.
- Your Critical-Task Action Plan should be at or near completion.
- The Relevant-Task Action Plan should be ready to implement. It clearly identifies other important tasks that must be reassigned now and in the near future.
- The busy-work notations in your journal should have opened your eyes to where you and your core team are currently spending too much time. There will never be a better opportunity to pare down this list. You will not be one hundred percent successful, but you can make some significant inroads.
- The under-performers who will make up your first group of employees to go through the model should now be identified.
- You have set a date to sit down with your core team to discuss their role in the transition.
- You have earmarked a date for introducing Quadrant Leadership to everyone in your company.

This chapter has been about identifying where you currently spend your time. Your transition journal either confirmed what you already knew or opened your eyes to just how much of your time is being spent away from protecting the core values of your brand. The first step to reducing busy-work is to acknowledge that it exists.

Some of this wasted time will begin to disappear as you use the model to turn around many of your under-performers. Just by raising their contribution to the company, you are reducing the amount of firefighting that has contributed to the eighty percent of activities that fall under the busy-work umbrella.

The Critical Task and Relevant Task action plans will go a long way to generating the free and flexible time that is essential for a successful transition. Your motivation must lie in your personal belief in what Quadrant Leadership can do for your employees, and for your business. The next step is to sit down with your core team to discuss their role in your company under Quadrant Leadership.

Integrating Your Core Team into Quadrant Leadership

Launching the Quadrant Leadership Model will require some serious support. Your core team already plays an important role in the daily operations of your business. Whether you call them managers, supervisors, charge staff, team leaders or something else, these are the people who typically oversee other employees in your business. A successful transition is heavily dependent on their willingness to embrace the principles that drive Quadrant Leadership. They must be kept abreast of everything you are doing to prepare for your transition. They will have many questions and will look to you for the answers.

In Meetings Versus Power Briefings, I will introduce you to an outstanding alternative to the traditional meeting. While I consider the majority of meetings to be a poor use of time, there is one type that when properly implemented can be highly effective.

A single focus meeting that deals exclusively with one theme or specific topic can be worthwhile. If you are successful at keeping the agenda tied specifically to a single theme, it will go a long way to reinforcing your message. Here is an example of an agenda for a single focus meeting that could be used to introduce Quadrant Leadership to your management team.

Topic: Quadrant Leadership
- What is Quadrant Leadership and what can it do for our company
- Introduction of the four quadrants and the role they play in raising employee performance and personal accountability expectations
- Transitional Journal discussion
- Busy-work discussion
- Review of the Critical Task Action Plan and assignment of specific tasks
- Review of the Relevant Task Action Plan and assignment of specific tasks
- Discussion of the first group to go through the model and why they were chosen
- Initial strategy discussion for the introduction of Quadrant Leadership to all of your employees

The agenda for a single focus meeting should be action-orientated. Everyone in the room will be expected to be fully engaged in every discussion, and the implementation of actionable strategies. It is important that each talking point on the agenda be allocated a specific amount of time. This will keep the meeting flowing smoothly and act as an incentive to stay focused.

In preparing for your meeting, I recommend that each participant read Quadrant Leadership in Sixty Seconds. They can access a copy from my website **darvillconsulting.com** by downloading the free sample of the opening chapters to The Entrepreneur's Apprentice. The more familiar they are with the philosophy that drives Quadrant Leadership and many of the concepts, principles and strategies designed to improve employee performance, the more productive your meeting is likely to be.

The first item on the agenda of any single focus meeting should introduce the topic and identify the specific purpose for the meeting. It should answer important questions like, why are we here, what do we hope to accomplish, and how will we be able to measure our success?

An overview of the quadrant templates is a great starting point. It will give your managers a general idea of how the model works. Use this time to talk about some of the many ways that Quadrant Leadership differs from traditional methods of employee development. A good place to start is with the three levels of certification right up to the role that Certified Skills Trainers play in the first quadrant as your technical subject matter experts.

Talk about the importance of self-initiative attributes and how they lead to increased accountability and ownership. Look at the role character plays in Quadrant Leadership. Explain 'team-thinking first' and how it reinforces the importance of team-building to increase performance and personal accountability to team initiatives.

From these discussions, your managers should begin to get a sense of how these aspects of employee development have the potential to make their job a whole lot easier in the future. If that doesn't generate some excitement, I'm not sure what will. When addressing the mentorship quadrant, let them know that it is based on relationship building and will take time to become part of the process.

Your next point of discussion will be your Transition Journal. Completing this was a major undertaking that required a great deal of effort on your part. Hopefully, you found it to be a worthwhile exercise. The knowledge you gained should give you some confidence in where to place your priorities as you transition into the model. Keep your journal discussion focused on the findings that directly affect your management team. If they did their reading, then they are familiar with the term busy-work, and the importance of the critical and relevant tasks that make up your action plans.

The first step in reducing busy-work is to become aware of when it is occurring. To help your managers understand the difference between busy-work and core activities, look at it from the perspective of the customer. If the action does not focus on meeting or exceeding customer expectations, there's a good chance that it is busy-work. You can also let them know that most busy-work activities are reactive rather that proactive in nature, such us as any example of firefighting.

Nothing on your agenda will prove to be more important than the implementation of your Critical and Relevant Task action plans. By assigning these important tasks to qualified members of your core team, you are taking a major step towards creating the free and flexible time that the model is going to demand from you. Your action plans include a time allotment for training and a specific date by which each of these tasks officially changes hands. It is important that the people you have chosen for these tasks feel your sense of trust in them. There will be no room for second-guessing.

In Quadrant Leadership, we teach the importance of earning trust. Trust plays a crucial role in every employee's ability to earn future independence. Your managers must feel your total confidence in their ability to be good stewards when it comes to taking care of these critical responsibilities.

The next item on your agenda is to identify the employees who will be the first to go through the model. This would be an excellent time to introduce Pareto's Law and discuss how it applies to this decision. By choosing the employees who are currently contributing the least to your company, you are testing the validity of the 80/20 rule. As a team, you should be able to come to a group consensus on the final list of names that will make up your inaugural group of candidates for the model.

It is important to note that outside of these closed discussions, these employees should never be referred to as the under-performers. This supports the principle of mutual respect that the model is built upon. It is critical that your managers' behavior mirrors yours when it comes to treating every employee with mutual respect. This is critical to achieving buy-in from your most skeptical critics.

The event that will introduce Quadrant Leadership to your entire team will be a major affair. Your objective during your core team meeting should be to create a storyboard and put together an action plan, assigning specific tasks and completion dates. This is such an important event marking the official launch of the Quadrant Leadership into your company. It is essential that everyone at the table be fully involved in planning this event, from the strategy sessions, to the dry run, to the execution.

Hopefully, your enthusiasm for Quadrant Leadership has rubbed off on every member of your core team. Over the next few days, you should take the time to talk with each of them individually. See how they are feeling about what is about to take place, and make a commitment to keep them totally involved in everything you are doing. Whether they realize it or not, they are critical to your success. The role they will play in the transition phase is just the beginning. If you have their full support, you have nothing to fear. A team that lives and breathes synergy is a formidable force. The odds are in your favor that you will have a smooth transition into Quadrant Leadership.

The Main Event

This is an exciting time for you and your company. Hopefully, you had an excellent meeting with the key players on your core team, and everyone is on board. The time has come to introduce Quadrant Leadership to the rest of your employees. This is your opportunity to share your vision for the future of your company and your passion for this approach to leadership. You must go boldly forward and never look back.

This is the kind of meeting that reaches the status of an event. There will be a lot of material to cover, and it will all come down to how you go about getting your message across. I have a few suggestions for you, but you should own this meeting. Your thoughts and ideas should be all over it. If you are successful, the majority of your employees will be looking forward to what Quadrant Leadership can do for them.

A successful single themed event should contain these five key elements.

- Action orientated material
- A strong delivery system
- Precision planning and execution
- Active participation
- A solid retention value

Here are a few suggestions for creating a great event.

1. Stir up interest before the meeting even begins.

Post messages around the room that have something to do with Quadrant Leadership. Examples might include, 'personal development for all,' or 'detailed thinkers versus concept thinkers,' or 'team-thinking first,' or 'fixed versus variable costs.' Build the level of curiosity. As your employees arrive for the meeting, let them walk around the room and try to figure out what all these messages mean.

2. Make the event fun.

Anytime you can combine entertainment with education; you dramatically improve your chances for success. I have always found that a well thought-out game is an excellent way to accomplish this task. You might even consider having the messages that you placed around the room incorporated into your game. Your objective is to share the important information that your employees will need to know prior to your transition.

A simple way to make sure you get a good cross-section of employees on each team is to use something I call the jigsaw selection method. As part of the preparation for your meeting, get someone to take a few colorful pages out of a glossy magazine and cut them into pieces of different shapes and sizes. The number of pieces cut from one page represents the number of people who will play on that team. Mix up all of the pieces before you hand them out. When it's time for everyone to get into their teams, have them stand and seek out the other pieces to their puzzle. A prize for the first team to finish is a sure-fire way of ramping up the participation level.

3. Make your meeting interactive

The last thing you want to do is stand at a podium and preach to the masses. You will quickly lose your momentum. Make your opening comments brief but powerful. Your words and the way you deliver them will set the tone for everything to follow. This is your opportunity to share your passion for Quadrant Leadership with your employees. There should be no doubt in their minds that you strongly believe in what you are about to do. The rest of the meeting should involve a free-flowing exchange of information and ideas, and plenty of two-way communication.

4. Encourage questions

Whether you intend to dedicate a specific part of your meeting to a Q+A session, or you simply plan to address questions as they arise, it's important that your employees feel that they can express themselves. This will give you an opportunity to tackle any concerns and make sure your employees have accurate information.

5. A full dry run is critical

I can't tell you how many meetings and presentations I've attended over the years that ended up being a disaster, simply because no one took the time to do a proper full-length dry run. The timing and pace of your meeting is important. It's crucial to start and end on time. A proper dry run will accurately test how much time each part of your meeting is taking. The only thing worse than a bad meeting is a bad meeting that runs long.

The dry run should also be used to check every piece of equipment and support material. There is no excuse for a poor-quality sound system or visuals or any other mishap that could derail what could have been a great meeting. Once you are underway, there will be no time to correct your mistakes.

Part of your dry run must include a live rehearsal for anyone who intends to speak. No matter how polished a presenter is, they need to practice. In my mind, there is nothing worse than a speaker who tells you that they are just going to say a few words and then shows up to the meeting completely unprepared. The introduction to Quadrant Leadership is such an important meeting. It deserves the time and attention that good preparation will guarantee.

A successful meeting does not necessarily mean that you have won over every employee. There are likely to be some skeptics in the crowd. The under-performers, who will go through the model first, are going to be suspicious of your motives. Some of them will view Quadrant Leadership as an elaborate gotcha tool rather than a personal development opportunity.

Skepticism is healthy and should never be discouraged. In the end, it will be up to you to walk the talk. So far, all your employees have heard is the talk. When they get a chance to experience the caliber of training and development that takes place in the Quadrant Leadership Model, it will go a long way to dispel the uncertainty.

Your breakthrough will come when your under-performers begin to turn around. They will prove that it is never too late to start again. Once they begin to put their trust in your hands, extraordinary things will start to happen.

This is a good time to address the subject of favoritism. It is human nature to like some people more than others, but bad practice to allow it to influence your behavior. The problem with favoritism is how it makes everyone else feel. You may think you are concealing it well, but there are many tells including body language, facial expressions, tone of voice, and eye contact. Your employees are not blind to blatant favoritism. If they sense that your commitment to equal opportunity for all has a hollow ring, you will begin to lose credibility, and word will spread quickly. The bottom line is this: if you do have favorites, make sure you keep it to yourself.

There is an awful lot riding on this meeting. You are only going to get one shot at this, so you need to make sure you get it right. Start with a storyboard that is both entertaining and informative. Make sure every member of your core team participates in the process. From the first strategy session to the full dry run, to the actual event, you need everyone to participate.

***

Quadrant Leadership has the ability to deliver on many levels. While the model is a highly effective tool, it's your commitment to lead through the power of insight and influence that will define your success. There will be many unanticipated hurdles along the way, some more serious than others. Never let these get you down. If something doesn't work, chalk it up to experience, and then pick yourself up and try something else. You will find that the model is an extremely flexible tool. Quadrant Leadership is more than capable of delivering some extraordinary results if you are prepared to persevere and see it through. The most important thing you can do for yourself, and for your employees, is to protect your time. Leading through knowledge rather than managing through constant direction can only happen if you are prepared to live it every day.

Part Four
The Four Quadrants

Quadrant One The Trainer / Expert	**114**
The Road to Certification	116
Detailed Thinkers versus Concept Thinkers	121
Quadrant Two The Teacher / Philosopher	**128**
Universal Truths of Employment	132
Self-Initiative Attributes	136
Cell Phones and Busy-Work	141
Business and the Bottom Line	145
Character and Self-Reflection	151
Quadrant Three The Observer / Coach	**156**
The Art of Coaching	159
Praising Without Conditions	165
The Search for a More Efficient Company	170
Team Thinking First	178
Quadrant Four The Mentor / Advisor	**182**
The Principle of Influence	184
A Matter of Trust	187
It's Okay, It's Not Okay, It's Never Okay	193

"No one learns as much about a subject
as one who is forced to teach it."
–Peter F. Drucker

Quadrant One
The Trainer / Expert

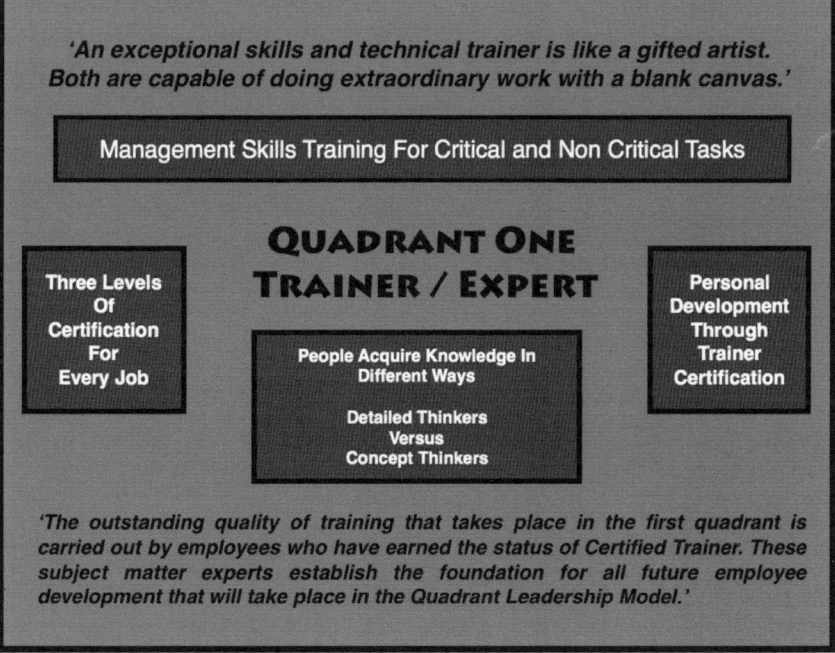

The only thing scarier than a micro-manager,
is a micro-manager who can talk and text at the same time.

The Road to Certification

The first quadrant is all about skills and technical training. Most companies have a solid training program in place that does not need to be reinvented to work with Quadrant Leadership. The majority of skills training is conducted by top performers who are very good at what they do. They are the subject matter experts who are more than capable of demonstrating the technical aspects of the job proficiently. Many businesses have a set of dedicated trainers who take care of all of the basic training for their company.

With Quadrant Leadership, we take a slightly different approach by including Trainer Certification as one of the levels of personal development. The three levels of certification are introduced on day one, and every new employee understands that their goal is to become certified at every level.

Our first objective is to exceed every new employees expectations. With Quadrant Leadership, the caliber of employee development that is the hallmark of the model is established in the first quadrant. Your Certified Skills Trainers lay a solid foundation by setting the bar extremely high. By the time your new employee is ready to move on to the second quadrant, they are more than ready to enter the next phase in their development journey.

You do not need to change any of the material you currently use for skills training. All you need to do is to add the certification process into your current program. If you already have a solid certification process in place, then you should work with that. If it ain't broke, don't fix it.

There are three levels of certification, and each has specific requirements. I never worried about fixed time frames when it came to certification. Getting it right is far more important than being able to check something off a to-do list. Some people learn at a much faster pace than others. This is perfectly fine, providing they do not miss important details that are critical to doing an excellent job. Traditional training programs tend to allocate the same amount of training time for every employee. One of the advantages of having free and flexible time is that it gives you the latitude to take a step back and revisit some of the basic training if you feel there is a need for it.

The best way to establish the importance of certification is to make it hard to earn. Giving someone a free pass for the sake of moving them on only serves to diminish your credibility and that of the certification process.

Certification serves many important purposes. It represents the level of proficiency that the employee has achieved. It allows us to celebrate their success. It suggests a minimum expectation for future performance. Higher levels of certification increase an employee's credibility and allow for more earned autonomy. It signals to their peer group that they have climbed higher up the trust ladder.

Visible certification allows the employee to proudly display their accomplishments. Attractively colored pins that can be worn on a lapel or collar celebrate the level of certification that the employee has achieved. Whether you choose to incorporate a visual aspect or not, the certification process plays a very important role in acknowledging progressive development.

The first goal for every new employee is to reach their first level of certification. The time frame to get there will vary, but speed is not the priority. The objective is to get it right. When an employee does earn their certification, it signals that they have reached a significant plateau in their development. Consistency is an important factor to earning certification. The employee does not need to be a superstar, but they do need to perform to the best of their ability on a regular basis.

Certification is celebrated every time it occurs. It really is a big deal. In the case of new employees, this is your first opportunity to recognize their accomplishment in front of their peer group.

The pride they feel in achieving their first level of certification will inspire them to keep going. Their success is your team's success, so encourage everyone to offer their congratulations. The new employee will quickly learn that their future success will depend on the kinds of relationships they forge with their fellow employees.

The foundation for certification begins in Quadrant I. It continues in the next two quadrants where *Self-Initiative Attributes* are incorporated into the development process. In our review of the second and third quadrant, we will explore many different basic and advanced self-initiative attributes that, when combined with skills training, significantly raise the employee's level of proficiency.

Requirements for Certification Level I

> The employee has acquired the skills to execute the fundamentals of their job description at a high level of proficiency. Verified in Quadrant I by a Certified Trainer
>
> The employee demonstrates how to incorporate *'Basic Self Initiative Attributes'* on a consistent basis. Verified in Quadrants II + III

An employee who has earned their second level of certification is considered to be highly skilled. They have demonstrated the ability to contribute consistently to the company in a significant way. This is an important achievement that deserves your praise and that of your management team. If you have chosen to incorporate a form of visual certification into your model, your employee will now have the privilege of displaying their well-earned recognition.

The next challenge for an employee who has been certified at level II is to become a certified trainer. One of the real strengths of Quadrant Leadership is that it challenges potential, rather than the requirements of a specific job. In doing so, we free ourselves from the confines of predetermined outcomes and established expectations.

Certification at level II represents a lot of hard work and a job well done. When you run into a situation where an employee has a level II certification and begins to underperform, you need to address the situation quickly. The ideal place to do this will be the fourth quadrant, but only if all of the elements of the mentor relationship are in place. The thing you know for certain is that this is not a developmental issue. The employee is under-performing for reasons that have nothing to do with their capability.

Situations like this must be addressed as soon as possible. If you can get your employee to open up, you have a good chance of turning the situation around. They have already given your company so much, so it is up to you to give them your best effort.

Requirements for Certification Level II

> The employee demonstrates an ability to carry out the fundamentals of their job description at the level of a subject matter expert. Verified in Quadrant I by a Certified Trainer
>
> The employee demonstrates an ability to work effectively in a team environment by successfully incorporating all of their Advanced Self Initiative Attributes into their scope of work to achieve optimum results. Verified in Quadrants II and III

Certified Trainers are incredibly valuable employees. Not only do they perform consistently at a high level, but they also set an outstanding example for how to do it right. The opportunities within your company will determine where these employees go next in their development journey. In the meantime, the role they currently play is critical to the success of Quadrant Leadership.

In the next chapter, we will explore something that most companies do not even consider when they begin the training process. It has to do with the way people learn. By taking into account the natural way that an individual processes information, we can create a training session that will work in tandem with how they absorb the new material. For an employee to reach their third level of certification, they must be able to grasp this very important concept and demonstrate how to use it to carry out a highly productive training session. This is just one more example of how we use Quadrant Leadership to its fullest potential. Even without your direct involvement, the training that your new employee is receiving from a Certified Skills Trainer far exceeds the norm.

Requirements for Certification Level III
Certified Trainer

The employee has demonstrated the ability to perform all of the requirements of the second level of certification at an outstanding level

The employee is a role model, skillfully using *'Advance Self Initiative Attributes'* to lead by example. Verified in Quadrants II + III

The employee is capable of incorporating the Detailed Thinker versus Concept Think exercise into their training sessions to enhance the overall learning experience. Verified in Quadrants II + III

Detailed Thinkers versus Concept Thinkers

One of my least favorite quotations suggests that *"those who can, do, and those who can't, teach."* I couldn't disagree more. Some of the most famous athletes in the world, Olympians and professionals alike, owe a great deal of their success to a dedicated team of coaches and trainers. Our school system is full of extraordinary teachers who inspire students to reach for the stars.

One of the reasons that I feel so strongly about Quadrant Leadership is because it delivers on so many levels. It demonstrates that you can be successful in business (I certainly was) by using the power of knowledge and insight to create an extraordinary team of extremely talented and highly proficient employees.

I think a better line might be,

"Those who can, do, and those who are willing to share their knowledge, do so much more."

Great trainers, like great teachers, play a vital role in the development of your employees. Your Certified Skills Trainers lay the foundation for everything that will follow. To achieve level III certification, a trainer cannot just be good at their job. There are millions of people who are good at what they do, but they are not good at showing someone else how to do it. A great trainer needs to be an excellent communicator and a good listener. By knowing a little about how a person thinks, a trainer can put together a far more productive training session. To achieve trainer certification, the employee must be able to grasp this concept and use it to their advantage when training new employees.

This skill requires a clear understanding of the concept, and a great deal of practice to effectively integrate it into the training process. Despite the degree of difficulty, in the Quadrant Leadership, every employee is expected to work towards their **trainer certification.** Some might feel that this is an unrealistic expectation. I hope you never permit yourself to think that way. Setting extraordinary expectations is one of the reasons why Quadrant Leadership is so effective. Will everyone get there? Probably not. The better question is, are they better off for trying? The answer is; absolutely!

After years of observation, I have concluded that the way people learn has a lot to do with the way they approach life in general. In other words, how they think and process information in their everyday lives is exactly how they learn. For the most part, people can be divided into two groups, the **detailed thinkers,** and the **concept thinkers.** I recognize that this might be considered over-simplification, but it can be useful when determining how to approach a training session.

Let's look at two different lists. The first examines the positive attributes of each type of thinker, the qualities that help them do their jobs well. The second explores attributes that are potential areas of opportunity for each type of thinker. This exercise can offer valuable insight when it comes to determining where to place emphasis during a training session.

None of this is absolute. In fact, everybody has some of the attributes common to both lists. There are, however, dominant attributes, and they tend to influence the way we approach situations.

How do you know what kind of thinker your new employee is? Start by showing them the list that displays the strengths common to both types of thinkers and ask them which list more closely aligns with the way they think and process information. It's not necessary to show them the opportunity list. You do not want your employee feeling that there is something wrong with the way they think. The trainer will utilize the second list to watch for potential areas of opportunity that may need to be addressed. Never assume that an employee has to display any of these attributes. You can download copies of both lists by visiting **www.darvillconsulting.com**.

Let's have a look at them now. It's important to remember that both types of thinkers have the potential to be great employees.

Detailed Thinker Strengths	Concept Thinker Strengths
• Their attention to details is excellent	• Instinctively look for a quicker or more efficient way to do things
• Methodical step by step approach to problem solving	• Have an uncanny ability to see the bigger picture without the need for all of the details
• Strong ability to focus	
• Follow instructions very well	• Free thinkers. Constantly on the look for creative solutions
• Use checklist and to do list effectively	• Would rather lead than follow. High energy level
• Function well in a structured environment	• Not afraid to make decisions that rely on gut instinct
• Even keeled demeanor Tend to stay calm under pressure	• Accepts risk as a reality of decision making
• Not easily distracted from the task at hand	

Detailed Thinker Opportunities

- Can be so focused on details that they miss the obvious

- Can become rattled in a crisis situation

- Do not like to make snap decisions. Can sit on the fence for too long

- Are uncomfortable relying on their gut instinct

- Prefer to follow rules than work outside of them

- Multi-tasking unrelated tasks is not their strongest suit

- Take longer to place trust in others

Concept Thinker Opportunities

- Can easily miss details that are crucial to problem solving

- Often act before they think, following instructions is not their strongest suit

- Can be blindsided by a lack of preparation

- Can jump to conclusions far too quickly

- Lack of focus can cause chaos

- Can be excitable and lose their calm in a crisis situation

- Lack of active listening skills can lead to missing crucial information

You can see how having this kind of information gives a trainer a better idea of how a particular individual receives and processes information. Taking into account the way people learn is just one more example of the quality of training that takes place in the Trainer / Expert Quadrant.

Imagine for a moment a terrible snowstorm. Two men have important jobs at the airport authority. One is an air traffic controller while the other is in charge of customer relations for the entire airport. Now imagine that it is late at night. Several flights have been canceled, and several incoming flights are trying to land. There are hundreds of unhappy travelers who are tired and frustrated.

Both men are very capable and extremely good at their jobs. Can you see how their natural approach to gathering information made each of them an excellent candidate for a particular job? An air traffic controller must follow detailed protocol to ensure the safety of every takeoff and landing. A customer service rep must be able to think outside of the box to do whatever it takes to make the best of a bad situation. Based on the strengths exercise, it is easy to figure out which thinker would be better suited for each job. Let's not lose sight of the fact that despite their obvious strengths, each type of thinker has areas of opportunities that need to be addressed to become excellent at what they do.

With new employees, it might seem obvious to focus on their strengths to create a good training session, but the trainer may want to take a different approach. Their strengths will likely shine through without much encouragement on the part of the trainer. We need to go back to our good friend Pareto and the 80/20 rule. Look for the elements that are likely to yield the highest return for the time invested. By focusing on the areas where opportunity exists, a certified trainer can make the greatest contribution to the employee's development. It should go without saying that we should also be praising their strengths at every opportunity.

Do you have an idea what camp I was born and raised in? Let's think about it. I hate having to fuss over details, and I have been known to step so far out of the box that I can no longer see it. The reality is, to reach the highest levels of proficiency you must accept that you need to work on the areas that are not your strengths to grow and be successful.

When I first trained my managers on the administrative side of the business, I needed to be a subject matter expert and have first-hand knowledge of every detailed aspect of the accounting principles to which all businesses must adhere. Without that expertise, I could never have shared that information with my managers and the audit that occurred that fateful rainy day would have been a total disaster. Even though detail is not my favorite thing, I can no more escape it than anyone else.

The bottom line is that we need both types of thinkers to make a business successful, and each can learn a great deal from the other.

Quadrant Two
The Teacher / Philosopher

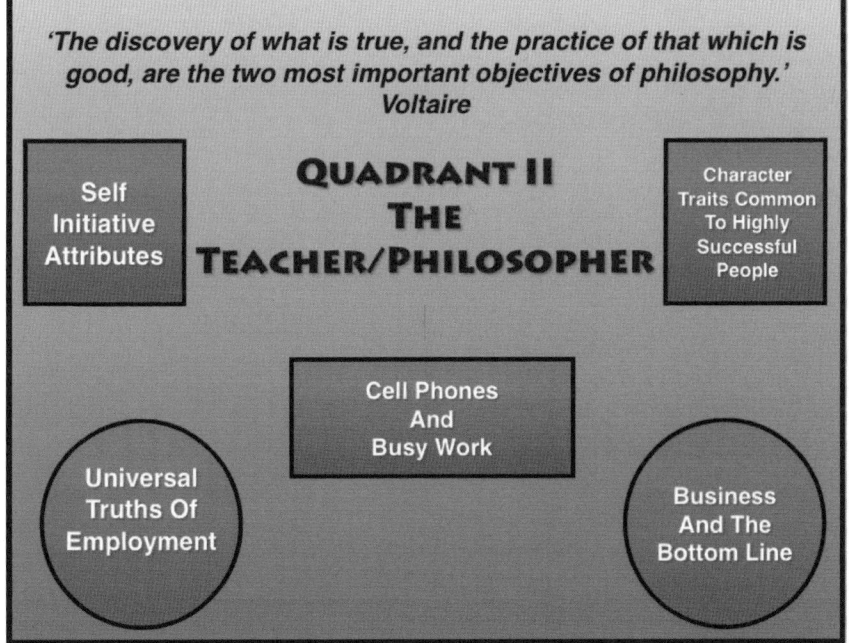

'The secret to bringing out the best in others is to start with yourself.'

The Teacher / Philosopher Quadrant marks the beginning of the second phase of employee development. This is the quadrant of two-way communications. Some of the discussions that take place here are serious in nature, beginning with *the Universal Truths of Employment*. This is such an important topic because it provides the new employee with a reality check of what it means to take on the responsibilities associated with being employed. Other sessions are far more relaxed, allowing for a free-flowing exchange of thoughts and ideas. Philosophy plays an important role in the second quadrant. As Voltaire suggests, philosophical discussions take us on a journey to seek out that which is true and to identify the things that are good for both the employee and for the business. Personally, I loved these highly entertaining exchanges of thoughts and ideas. I learned never to underestimate an individual's contribution based solely on their age. Some of my favorite memories are of spirited philosophical debates with sixteen-year-old employees.

This quadrant continues the layering of knowledge that the model was designed to deliver. Your employees have received some excellent skills training in the first quadrant. Now they will begin to explore some concepts and principles that are less tangible, but equally as important to their development. Your quest to build an army of highly proficient brand builders has just begun.

For many of your employees, this transition period marks the first time they become fully engaged in a personal one-to-one session with you. This is a new experience for both of you, and there are bound to be some challenges along the way. Newer employees will adapt quickly. Their opinions of you and the company they work for are in flux. Most of your new hires will view this kind of personal attention favorably, and they will look forward to what lies ahead. Make sure to let them know what they can expect when the two of you move to the third quadrant. **The full cycle of development** that takes place in the first three quadrants will allow your employees to earn their certification. This is a time for great celebration and praise. Your employee gets to experience first-hand the sense of pride that comes from real accomplishment. As more of your employees complete their first certification, you will start to see extraordinary changes begin to take place in your company.

For your more experienced employees, a lot will depend on the relationship that currently exists between you. Some of the under-performers will be wary of your motives. Other longer-term employees may have opinions of you that leave them less than excited at the prospect of spending more time together. Do not be discouraged by these views. You must have faith in the power of Quadrant Leadership to do its job.

As long as you are fully committed to providing every employee equal quality development time, then you will have met your commitment. The rest will be left up to the employee. Since the second quadrant is where we encourage open discussion, any doubts or misgivings that exist should be addressed right away. Make it clear that your goal is to see every employee achieve their true potential in your company. As long as they are prepared to meet you halfway, you look forward to watching them succeed.

For me, these were my greatest victories. Turning around an employee who was headed in the wrong direction and seeing them make a significant contribution to the company made the failures so much easier to take. Each time I witnessed this kind of turn-around, it would strengthen my belief in Quadrant Leadership and its powerful mission statement: *Leading through the power of knowledge, rather than managing through the drone of repetitive direction.*

The effort you put into these first sessions will be critical to your future success with the rest of your employees. For total buy-in to take place, these first employees must see some real value in the time you invest in them. They must believe that you genuinely want them to succeed. If you have done your job well, it will not be long before they are singing the praises of Quadrant Leadership.

Universal Truths of Employment

One of my favorite tasks was to write letters of reference for employees who were moving on. These letters were a testament to the success of Quadrant Leadership, and I never grew tired of writing them. I never understood bosses who got angry with good employees who gave fair notice informing them that they would soon be leaving. It is just one of the realities of business. People move on for a variety of reasons. I suspect the anger is more likely directed at themselves for not being prepared for the departure of a key player. The beauty of Quadrant Leadership is that it is always preparing other employees to take over when someone decides to leave. The most we can ever expect from any employee is to make a positive contribution to our company. If they have done their part, then it's up to us to do ours. We owe it to them to write a glowing letter of reference.

A strong reference letter can be the deciding factor in your employee's ability to secure a good job at their next place of employment. Your employees need to know on day one just how important it is that they make the kinds of decisions that will guarantee them your praise when they decide to move on.

Many young people who are entering the job market for the first time have no idea what they are getting themselves into. All they see is a paycheck. They have no concept of what it means to take on the responsibilities associated with employment.

The second quadrant is where two-way communication gets underway. It is critical that your new employees clearly understand what will be expected of them. There are some *Universal Truths of Employment* that every employee should be familiar with. These truths will help them to prepare for their future in your company. This information is so important that you will want to have this conversation during your first one-to-one session in the Teacher / Philosopher Quadrant.

No employee should be spared this list, regardless of their employment history. These universal truths are timeless and are worth sharing with every person who joins your company. My guess is that the majority of new hires with previous work experience will tell you that they have never had this kind of discussion with an employer before.

Keep in mind when adding or deleting things from your list that every truth should be universal in nature and apply to virtually any type of employment. Do not confuse policy statements with universal truths. This list should remain generic but clearly illustrate to your new employee what will be required of them to be successful in your company.

If you tend to hire a lot of youth, as I did, I suggest that you encourage your new employees to take the list home and review it with their parents. Your objective is to leave no doubt in anyone's mind that there is no difference in the expectations set for a young part-time student and those of a full-time professional.

If a parent takes exception to something on your list, now is the time to address it to avoid conflict in the future. You can download a copy of the Universal Truths of Employment by going to **www.darvillconsulting.com**.

Universal Truths of Employment

1. **Nobody owes you a job. It is up to you to earn it and then to keep it.** Your education, qualifications, and experience might get you an interview, and they may ultimately land you the job, but to be successful in business, you must be prepared to prove your worth every day. Consistency is a far more important attribute to an employer than moments of excellence.

2. **Nobody starts at the top or anywhere near it.** You will have to climb the promotional ladder just like everyone else. When you begin to show your worth to your employer, opportunities will start to open for you. The majority of successful businesspeople started at or near the bottom, and there is absolutely nothing wrong with that.

3. **Your job is to make money for your company.** Profit is the lifeblood of every business. Without profit, there is no company and no need for you. A profitable company is a healthy company with plenty of opportunity for potential advancement.

4. **Every job in the company is important, and no job is beneath you.** If the day comes when you believe that you are better than the job you do, you have stayed one day too long.

5. **Theft is theft is theft.** There is no excuse or circumstance that will justify taking that which was never yours to begin with. No matter how you try to rationalize it in your mind, it is wrong, and you have only yourself to blame for the consequences you face.

6. **No employer is looking for an average performer.** If your intent is to do an average job, then you deny yourself the opportunity to grow. If the people around you are being promoted, and you are not, the first person you need to have a talk with is yourself.

7. **The attitude that 'it's only a part time job' is an insult to you.** You must believe that the contributions you make to your company are just as important as any full-time employee. Never embrace this kind of thinking and never accept it from anyone else.

8. **If you lie to your employer, it will eventually catch up with you.** Missing shifts, calling in sick to get out of work, and showing up late are hardly the habits of winners. One of the best things your boss will do for you one day is to write a letter of reference, singing your praises. That piece of paper can be worth its weight in gold. You deserve it, so make smart choices and earn it.

9. **You can't expect to be paid more and do less.** A promotion can earn you more money, but it comes with more responsibility. If you are not prepared to do the work, don't ask for the raise.

10. **Not all employers are created equal.** You are likely to work for several bosses in your lifetime. They may run the gambit from the great to the terrible. If you happen to find a boss that is prepared to invest their time in you, then do your part and rise to the occasion.

Self-Initiative Attributes

Discussions that address **self-initiative attributes** are approached in an entirely different manner to skills training. This deals with concepts and principles rather than clear, tangible actions. It is important that every employee is able to integrate self-initiative attributes into their job description to function at a higher level of proficiency. By reviewing the attributes you consider the most important for your business with your employee, you are taking the first step towards promoting independent thinking. Concepts as fundamental as personal accountability and proactive decision-making are extremely important and play a critical role in future development. Finger pointing is not an acceptable practice in Quadrant Leadership. Once they take full accountability for their actions, they will see that making a poor decision is still better than making no decision at all.

Your first one-to-one session on this subject will begin by introducing each of the basic self-initiative attributes to your employee and discussing their importance. As they demonstrate their ability to integrate these skills effectively into their job description, you move on to the more advanced initiatives. This second group of attributes explore the power of team synergy. They offer the employee some very important insight into how much more can be accomplished by a high functioning, well connected team working together to achieve common goals.

In the third quadrant, we encourage our employees to exercise their self-initiative attributes to make important decisions. The model is not theory-driven. Quadrant Leadership uses real world situations to test these attributes, recognizing that mistakes are likely to happen. As long as your employee shows a willingness to learn from their personal experiences, each mistake they make will ultimately serve to strengthen their future performance.

Incorporating basic self-initiative attributes into the employee's job description is the next step in the continuous development process that takes place in Quadrant Leadership. While these concepts and principles will come naturally to some employees, others will struggle with making the kinds of decisions that allow them to earn your trust and their future independence. The flexibility built into the model allows you to approach development opportunities from virtually any quadrant. If you have successfully guarded the time you will need to implement the model; you will have the freedom to extend any session you deem necessary. If you truly believe the time you invest in your employees will ultimately pay off, you will never watch the clock when doing so.

The majority of traditional training models do not allow for this kind of flexibility. Information tends to travel in one direction and in most cases, there is a finite amount of time for the employee to absorb the content and demonstrate their ability to execute. In the Quadrant Leadership Model, we work alongside our employees and the dialogue continues to flow freely. Our primary goal is to make certain that the employee has a firm grasp of the material, and how it will help them to do their job extremely well.

There will be times when you start a session in the second quadrant, only to realize that the employee is more than ready to show what they are capable of. When shifting into the third quadrant you will be using coaching techniques that are intended to support your employee as they attempt to demonstrate their ability to perform at a significantly higher level of proficiency. The term 'real-time observation' refers to a collective set of highly effective coaching strategies that are used in real world situations to support your employee's development. These sessions have nothing to do with inspecting or critiquing. The third quadrant invests whatever amount of time is necessary for the employee to integrate the things they have learned in the first two quadrants into their job description.

In this case, the employee has been successful in blending basic self-initiative attributes with their skills expertise. This accomplishment will move them one step closer to achieving their first level of certification. One of the most important considerations in awarding certification is the employee's ability to perform consistently at this new level of proficiency. We are not looking for moments of brilliance. Consistency is an extremely important part of the development equation.

Let's take a look at some examples of basic self-initiative attributes. This list is far from definitive, but acts as an example of the kinds of things you may include on your list.

Basic Self-Initiative Attributes for Level One Certification

11. **Personal Accountability** - Full acceptance that the decisions we make, as well as those we fail to make, are of our own volition. In Quadrant Leadership, we make it clear that finger-pointing is not an acceptable option for relieving one's self from accountability. Meaningful growth cannot occur until we are prepared to take full ownership for our actions.

12. **Scope of Work** - For the basic level, the employee's accountability is tied to their personal job description. The employee clearly understands that they will be responsible for implementing the self-initiative attributes that enhance their personal scope of work.

13. **Short-Term Decision Making** - Taking the initiative to make quick decisions that will effectively address immediate situations before they rise to a crisis level, without the need for direct supervision.

14. **Long-Term Decision Making** - Anticipating barriers and issues through experience and knowledge. Looking for and applying longer-term solutions to situations that occur within the employee's personal scope of work.

15. **Multi-Tasking** - Assessing and executing tasks that can be done in tandem to optimize efficiency.

16. **Time-Planning and Prioritizing** - Clear understanding of how preparation and execution work to make the best use of time. Demonstrating the ability to prioritize tasks and activities based on importance within the scope of work.

17. **Personal Work Ethic** - The level of intensity applied to execute the job at a high level of proficiency. The effort put forth should correspond directly with the urgency of the situation, without the need for direct supervision.

The nature of your own business will determine which specific self-initiative attributes are essential to support the core values of your brand. Keep in mind that your employees are not mind-readers. So many of the problems that occur in the workplace come from misunderstanding what is expected. Do not fall into the trap of saying that something should be obvious or common sense. I can tell you from experience that one person's version of common sense does not necessarily match someone else's. Stop assuming that something is a given. Make sure you are both on the same page. You can accomplish this by ensuring that your list of self-initiative attributes reflects all of your expectations.

***

Advanced Self-Initiative Attributes require the employee to have a greater understanding of the whole operation and how teamwork benefits the entire company. Many of the philosophical discussions that take place in the second quadrant are designed to help the employee gain a clearer understanding of the big picture and their role in it.

Team synergy requires the use of advanced self-initiative attributes. Before that can happen your employee must have a strong grasp of the basic self-initiative attributes that fall within their scope of work and can demonstrate their ability to integrate them successfully into their job description.

In the next chapter, I will introduce you to something I call team **thinking first**. In essence, it refers to the role that team synergy plays in creating outstanding brand identity. For your employee to earn their second level of certification, they must be able to demonstrate their ability to implement successfully advance self-initiative attributes that support the team as a whole.

Quadrant Leadership works extremely well in a team environment. The flexibility that is built into the model allows you to switch from a one-to-one session to a team session with ease. Remember that as a philosophy of business Quadrant Leadership is based on real world, here and now situations. If a team opportunity arises, then you should take full advantage of it.

Part of the challenge for your managers will be finding the right balance between when to provide specific direction, and when to allow each employee the opportunity to use their self-initiative attributes to address a situation. It can be frustrating for an employee when they attempt to take action, only to be redirected by a manager.

During your many discussions in the second quadrant, you must make sure that your employee clearly understands the role that management plays in your company. There will be many times when the employee will be required to follow a manager's direction, even when they feel that they would have made a better decision on their own. The overall goal of your management team is to serve the best interests of every customer. There will always be a need for a final decision maker and your employees must be able to respect that.

Earlier, we discussed how the role management plays will begin to shift as more employees move through the certification process. If your employees are doing an excellent job, and effectively using their self-initiative attributes, there is no need for excessive supervision. Until that happens, your managers will struggle to find the right balance. There are likely to be some bumps along the way, but take heart in knowing that it will get much better as more of your employees move through the model.

Cell Phones and Busy-Work

These are extraordinary times for advancements in technology. A business today has many new tools at its disposal to help manage costs, promote goods and services, and improve market share. Even brick and mortar companies have recognized the benefit of having a strong presence on the Internet.

Electronic messaging instruments like email and text messaging, together with social media platforms such as Facebook and Twitter, have transformed the way we stay connected. There are some obvious advantages to being able to send information anywhere in the world with the click of a button. Ironically, it is the simplicity of the medium, and the way we have become accustomed to reacting to it, that has created a new set of challenges for business. In many ways, electronic messaging has become the modern version of Pavlov's dog. More commonly referred to as conditioned response, it is the net result that occurs when a conditioned stimulus is paired with an unconditioned response.

The behavior was first studied by Ivan Pavlov who observed that when he held a piece of meat in front of a dog, it would immediately begin to salivate. He then began to ring a bell at the same time as he tempted the dog with the savory treat. It was not long before the sound of the bell alone could cause the dog to salivate.

In today's world, Pavlov's bell has been replaced by the familiar chirp or buzz that emanates from our cell phone each time a new text message or email arrives. For many people, the unconscious response is to reach immediately for their phone. In the blink of an eye, their focus shifts from the task at hand to the incoming message. Like Pavlov's dog, whose senses were stimulated by the sound of the bell, our need to know who sent us a message, and the content of the message, is so compelling that our focus immediately shifts.

This may be perfectly acceptable in our private lives, but for business, it can be counterproductive and highly disruptive. No other form of communication can shift our behavior so quickly. The fundamental key to success in business lies in our ability to stay focused on our core objectives. The ease at which electronic messaging can redirect an employee's attention away from the task at hand to something completely off topic is why I consider electronic messaging to be the *godfather of all busy-work*.

To prepare for your transition into Quadrant Leadership, you were asked to complete a daily journal over the period of an entire month. The purpose was to track how you are currently spending your time. You may have been surprised to discover how much of your time was taken by this medium.

At first glance, these messages might appear to be justified, given that many of them deal directly with some aspect of your business. To determine if they have had a positive or negative effect, ask yourself this simple but important question: Did these messages, and the time required to address them, support the core objectives of my business, or did they shift my focus to activities that were more aligned with someone else's priorities or some form of busy-work? Let me be clear here; both email and text messaging can be highly effective forms of communication for business, when used properly. Messages that assist your employee in delivering a better experience to the customer are a very good thing. To ensure a successful transition into Quadrant Leadership, it is imperative that you address the challenges that electronic messaging can present for your company.

Clearly, there are tremendous advantages to being able to get important information out quickly. As long as the medium maintains focus rather than creating distractions, it can be an outstanding tool for any business.

Three Things to Consider Before You Write Your Next Email or Send Your Next Text

- The subject matter should support the core objectives of your business. The content of the message will not shift the employee's focus away from the priorities of their job to some form of busy-work.

- The message should follow the same principles as a good power briefing by using easy to read bullet points that get straight to the point. A succinct recap page should be attached to any email that carries a lot of information. The reader can quickly determine if they should read the email in its entirety now, or if it can be left to be read when it's more convenient.

- The email or text message should only go to the employees that will directly benefit from the content. Unless otherwise specified, copying others who need to be kept informed should be limited to the bullet point recap page only.

Types of E-Communications to Look Out For

- Any internal text messages or email that clearly shifts your employee's attention away from their primary responsibilities.

- Any message from an outside source that is likely to infringe upon your time or your employee's time should be carefully scrutinized. There is no doubt that the sender considers their message to be important. The question is, important for whom? If it does not support the core initiatives of your business, then it falls under the busy-work umbrella. Steps should be taken to eliminate or reduce the number of these kinds of messages that reach your people.

- Micro-managing through emails and text messages does not support the Quadrant Leadership philosophy of leading through knowledge, rather than managing through constant direction. The objective of the model is to provide your employees with the business education and the tools they need to perform independently at a high level of proficiency. One of the key objectives of Quadrant Leadership is to encourage your employees to use their self-initiative attributes to make sound decisions without the need for excessive supervision. As the majority of your employees move through the model, the last person they need to encounter is a micro-manager.

- Watch for employees who avoid direct contact with other employees and use emails and text messages as their primary form of communication. Quadrant Leadership is all about mutual respect and team thinking first. It's extremely important that these kinds of situations are identified and resolved as quickly as possible.

- People issues of any kind should never be addressed through text messages or emails. There is no guarantee that any of this information will remain confidential.

Business and the Bottom Line

My approach to implementing the Quadrant Leadership Model was far less structured than you might think. Early on, I learned never to plan too far ahead. The fact that you are out there on a daily basis sharing the kind of knowledge that supports the growth and development of all of your employees is what gives the model its power. With Quadrant Leadership, we lead through knowledge rather than manage through direction. This is not a program, and you must do everything in your power to make sure it never becomes one. It is true that there is an administrative aspect, but try to resist the temptation to bury yourself in paperwork.

Whenever I was getting ready for a session that would cover a lot of information, I would prepare in exactly the same way as I would for a good power briefing. Short bullet points that are clear and concise will help you to organize your thoughts. Resist the temptation to build detailed development files on each employee. The purpose for your note-taking should be to give you a framework to continue your work. If you do find yourself spending a substantial amount of time on the paperwork side of Quadrant Leadership, you need to take a step back. The power of the model comes from the time spent with each employee. No amount of time allocated to paperwork will ever replace the time invested in a good productive session.

I always looked at it from the perspective of the customer. They could care less what words sit on a piece of paper in a filing cabinet. What is important to them is that you are fully committed to executing the promises of your brand. So many businesses are drowning in bureaucratic paperwork. Customers are not interested in performance evaluations. Their opinion is formed by their personal experience. If it was a positive experience, then in their minds, your employee did a good job. The twenty percent of things that really matter happen in the now. What happened yesterday and what will happen tomorrow are simply not your customer's concern.

The free and flexible time that you create for yourself will provide you with the freedom to resist over-structuring the model. There will be times when the subject matter you are dealing with is so important that the last thing you want to do is cut the session off simply because time is up. One of the things that makes Quadrant Leadership such a powerful development tool is the flexibility you give yourself to deal with any situation, working from any quadrant, regardless of the time it takes.

Not all subjects or developmental needs are created equal. Some of the things that you will cover are far more important than others. The time invested in these particular topics will pay higher dividends simply because the decisions that are required carry far greater consequences.

One example is the subject of profitability, and in particular, your employees' role in contributing to the bottom line. The approach I took to tackling this incredibly important topic was drawn from the lessons I learned while conducting those small business workshops many years earlier.

I knew that if I wanted my employees to make the kinds of decisions that would protect and grow the profitability of my restaurants, they needed to know a lot more about what goes into running a small business. The Quadrant Leadership Model gives us the perfect platform to prepare our employees for their role in creating a healthy bottom line.

In the *Universal Truths of Employment*, they are reminded that making money for the company is an integral part of their job. No business can hope to survive if it is losing money. I never missed an opportunity to tie some form of cost management into an employee session. The time invested in these types of discussions has the potential to return enormous dividends

I am not suggesting that you are sharing your actual profit and loss statement, or any other financial document, with your employees. Generic examples will work just fine. The objective is to show them just how many different costs go into making a small business function.

How much or how little of this side of the business you are willing to share with your employees is completely up to you. My experience taught me that the more eyes I had looking out for profit opportunities, the better the bottom line. Since the controllable section of the profit and loss statement is where your employees can make the greatest impact, it only makes sense that this is where you concentrate your effort.

The categories listed on a profit and loss statement can vary widely, depending on the industry and the nature of the business. Despite the many differences, most of the costs in the controllable section of the statement can be identified as either being **fixed** or **variable**.

Since fixed costs by definition cannot be improved upon, we focus on the fixed cost percentage instead. I used a simple exercise to demonstrate the important relationship between the fixed cost percentage and top line sales.

There are many more opportunities to improve profitability on the variable side of the equation, but I would always begin with the fixed cost discussion because it reinforced how important increasing market share is to optimizing profitability. This simple exercise illustrates how significantly the fixed cost percentage can be affected by rising or falling top line sales. Shrinking the fixed cost percentage is the first way our employees help us create a healthy bottom line.

Sales	Fixed Costs $	Fixed Cost %
$100,000.00	$23,000.00	23.0%
	5% growth in sales	
$105,000.00	$23,000.00	21.90%
	5% decline in sales	
$95,00.00	$23,000.00	24.21%

Most profit discussions will begin in the second quadrant. When addressing the fixed cost percentage, we talk about the employee's role in building sales. By executing the core values of your brand to the very best of their ability, they pave the way for the kind of market share growth that will minimize the impact that fixed costs have on the business. The more committed they are to creating outstanding brand identity, the more likely we are to see our top line grow and our fixed cost percentage shrink.

Variable costs, by definition, can be affected by several factors. The most common mistake many bosses make when it comes to addressing variable cost opportunities is that they limit their discussions to the really big ones. While Pareto's Law supports focusing first on the costs where the greatest savings can be achieved, there will come a time when those costs will be well under control. At that point, you should be looking for other opportunities. That is why it's important that your employees are familiar with all variable costs that can be found on the profit and loss statement.

For the restaurant industry, the food and beverage line items represent the single biggest variable expense and would logically be the first place to start. Food cost control is a delicate balance between raw food cost, portion control, waste management, and shrinkage while providing the customer with a quality finished product at a competitive price. It can be a challenge to maintain that balance when the restaurant is busy, and that is why it is so important that every employee understands what's at stake.

A huge part of maintaining excellent results is to make sure your employees are constantly kept informed about how the business is doing. The more information you can share with them that will validate a job well done, or target areas of opportunity, the more likely you are to achieve excellent results on a regular basis.

By listing and identifying all your variable costs on a generic profit and loss statement, you accomplish some important objectives. When your employees see how many different controllable costs go into running your business, they will quickly realize that the raw cost of an item is just one component of the costs that a business incurs. If you are able to make the important connection between employee decision-making and profitability, you will be well on your way to building a healthy bottom line.

You want your employees thinking about how their decisions affect all variable costs, not just the largest ones. The old adage 'a penny saved is a penny earned' was never truer than when it comes to effectively controlling variable costs. I have a great story that relates to one of my own employees who took the initiative to tackle a cost opportunity.

In the location where she worked, the dining room was surrounded by tall windows on three sides. On sunny days, the room was very bright, and on occasion, customers would complain about the glare. Having so many windows also meant that on the hottest days of the year, the air conditioning units would be working at full capacity.

One day she approached me after having done some extensive research. She told me she believed she had found a way to make the dining room more pleasant on a sunny day while improving energy efficiency. She had located a company that sold a high-quality UV film that could be fitted to any window. Not only did the manufacturer guarantee that it would eliminate glare, but they also claimed that it could repel heat and cut energy costs. They even suggested that many of their customers had seen their utility bill decrease by as much as twenty percent.

She put together a proposal that included the upfront costs to purchase the material and to have it professionally installed. She then calculated the time it would take to recoup the initial costs if we were able to achieve just a five percent savings on our overall utility bill during the hot summer months. She even projected future savings once the initial investment had been paid off. To say that I was impressed would be an understatement. I gave her permission to work with her manager to have the product installed.

I wish I could tell you that this story was an absolute home run, but like many things that sound a bit too good to be true, it was. That's not to say it was a mistake. The glare problem was eliminated completely, and many customers commented on how much nicer the dining room was on a sunny day. As far as the energy savings were concerned, we averaged about a two and a half percent reduction in costs during the summer months, a far cry from the potential twenty percent boldly suggested by the manufacturer.

It took a little longer to recoup the initial investment, and the long-term savings were minimal, but they were savings nonetheless. From my perspective, this was still a success story. Thanks to one eighteen-year-old employee, we were able to reduce a variable cost while improving the customer experience. Even though she felt she had failed, I assured her that this was not only a success, it was a total win/win.

The praise she received for her effort was well deserved, and it served to inspire other employees to come up with unique and interesting ways to reduce costs. My challenge was to explain why a particular idea was not likely to work without discouraging the employee from continuing to think outside the box. After all, they had a boss who spent half of his life outside the box.

The lesson here is simple. Your employees play an integral role in reducing your fixed cost percentage simply by protecting your brand and building market share. They are also the same people who are more than capable of managing all of your variable costs. The more they understand about the inner workings of a small business, the more they are able to contribute to creating a healthy bottom line.

Character and Self-Reflection

Many years ago, I met a man who would leave a lasting impression on my life. It has been nearly a decade since his passing, but his memory lives on. Brian Midgley was a gentleman, a humorist, and a compassionate human being. He left an extraordinary legacy on how to do things right.

I first met Brian and his wife Beryl through my former sister in law, Linda. She was soon to be engaged to the couple's only son, Russ. This was a family that was easy to like, and while I truly enjoyed Beryl's company, there was something about Brian that I immediately gravitated to. He had a way of making you feel like you were the most important person in the room. His ability to engage you in a conversation was like no one else I had ever met. With Brian, you always got the impression that he was genuinely interested in everything you had to say. He relished a good debate and was fascinated by different points of view. As far as Brian was concerned, differing opinions were to be expected, and each commanded the other's respect.

You never left a conversation with Brian that did not make you think. The welcoming sound of his voice and the easiness of his demeanor were his calling card. He saw no value in conflict and would often remind me that confrontation can only take place when there are two willing participants. To watch Brian in action was like witnessing a master class in the art of extraordinary people practices.

Brian was a banker by trade, and the contributions he made to his branch were significant. When I think of how much the banking industry has changed since his passing, I am reminded how the autonomy that a branch manager and a loans officer once enjoyed has been severely restricted. The tight controls and regulations that the entire industry subscribes to today pay lip service to customer loyalty and the whole notion of enduring relationships. The great irony is that these were the very qualities that made Brian such a successful businessman. His clients were genuinely happy with the way they were treated, and they knew he valued their business. In turn, they would share their experience with their family and friends, and the bank would be the beneficiary. This is the same institution that no longer allows their managers the autonomy to find creative solutions. I truly believe that Brian would have had no choice but to move on to a new vocation. His talents would have demanded it of him.

Many people attended his funeral. In addition, to family and friends, many former coworkers and even some of his competitors in the banking industry came to pay their respects. Several people spoke, and the theme was universal. This was a man of great integrity who was admired by so many people, for so many reasons.

Long after my divorce, we continued to talk on a regular basis. He was always interested in what I was up to, and I would often share with him a particular problem or a situation I was confronted with. Always the good listener, Brian would somehow manage to bring the conversation back around to the importance of respect in finding common ground. I never forgot his words, and I made it my mission to make sure that the Quadrant Leadership Model would rest on a foundation of mutual respect.

Positive character attributes can play such an important role in finding success in every aspect of our lives. For so many businesses, the only time the subject of character is addressed is when some aspect of an employee's character is affecting their performance in a negative way.

There is no doubt in my mind that as a youth, I would have benefited enormously from conversations that explored the positive character attributes that can enrich our lives. In the second quadrant, we tackle the subject head on. We talk about people who have positively influenced our employee's life. We ask them to tell us why they admire this person. What is their approach to addressing confrontation and challenging situations? Do others share your view on this person, and why? We explore positive character traits that are common to people who have the ability to influence outcomes. Why are they so successful? What is it that makes them so different?

Over the years, I had these kinds of discussions with many employees. While I would not have qualified any particular conversation as life changing, I can tell you that they got my people thinking about the role character can play in achieving success in every aspect of their lives. Despite spending the majority of my life working with youth, it is my profound belief that every employee, in any business, regardless of their age, can benefit from these types of discussion.

External dialogue is important, but the internal dialogue that takes place in the back of our minds is what makes these exchanges so unique. At some point in the conversation, we begin a natural progression towards self-reflection. We begin to question our character and how we might be viewed by others. While our outward appearance will not likely betray our thoughts, the value of these discussions is that they get us thinking.

Self-reflection, while personal, is a healthy exercise that each of us, at some point in our lives, must undertake if we truly want to grow and develop. As I was heading home from Brian's funeral that day, I could not help but wonder what people might say about me after I am gone. Would I be respected? Would I be celebrated as a decent human being? Would I make a positive impact on other people's lives? Would I be admired? I had no idea what the answers were, but there was one thing I did know for sure. Whether I was prepared to admit it to myself or not, it mattered.

The best thing about self-reflection is that it happens naturally without any need for provocation. Whether we are discussing personal integrity or credibility or the value of our word, or any other positive character attribute, the key is to allow our employees the opportunity to self-reflect and decide for themselves what is important.

It is easy to recognize good character qualities, but it is another matter to act upon them. As human beings, we are innately flawed. Each of us is unique, made up of a kaleidoscope of character traits. Not every aspect of our character is created equal. For most of us, there are elements of our character that are not necessarily our best qualities. Only we can decide what role these attributes will play in our future.

In the second quadrant, our discussions focus solely on positive character traits. There is no need to call an employee's character into question. Not only is it unwise, it is incredibly counter-productive. It would be viewed as a personal attack, and the credibility that you are attempting to build with your employee would be severely damaged

In the *Mentor Quadrant*, we have an opportunity to address specific character attributes that hinder the employee's ability to reach their full potential. Before we can go there, the unique qualities that this kind of relationship demands must be in place. Not every employee will participate in this quadrant, and you must learn to accept that.

You need to be able to exercise extraordinary patience when it comes to dealing with the complexities associated with a person's character. For those who are ready and willing to let you into their inner sanctum, there is much to gain. Until then, stay focused on discussions that reinforce the value of positive character attributes and make sure you continue to keep the dialogue alive.

In Quadrant Leadership, we frequently remind our employees that there is no room for finger pointing. With real growth comes a greater sense of personal accountability. Character building involves a willingness to take full responsibility for our actions, including all aspects of our behavior. I would often remind my employees that no one is perfect, and most of us will make some blunders in our lifetime. As long as we are prepared to accept the consequences of our actions and make amends for our mistakes, there will always be an opportunity to redeem ourselves and redefine who we are and what we stand for.

If no one aspires to be average, then the last thing we should do is settle for it.

Quadrant Three
The Observer / Coach

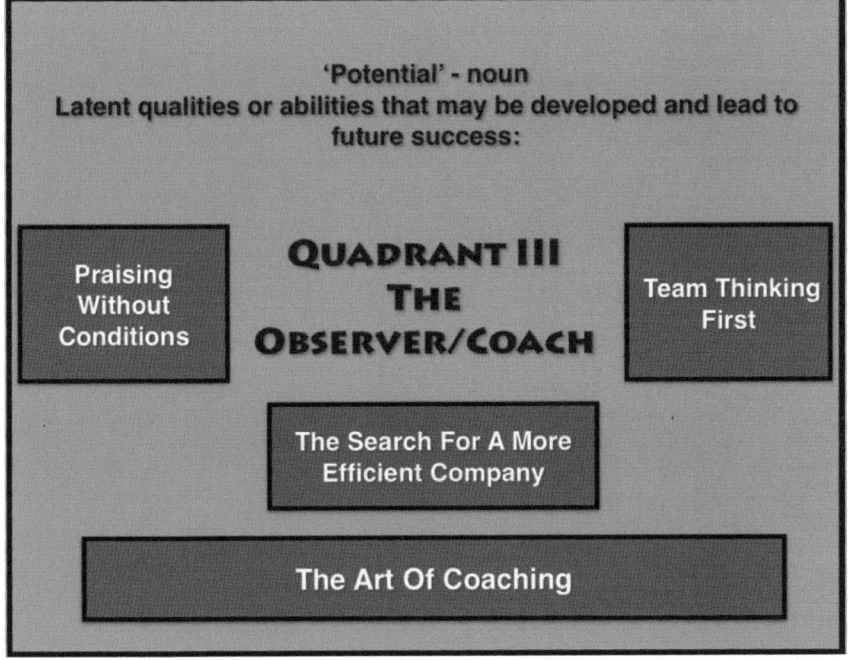

Welcome to the busiest quadrant of them all. In your role as the Observer / Coach, you have more freedom to decide how you will spend your time. What might begin as a one-on-one session can grow to include several employees. A critical part of every employee's development involves their ability to contribute in an effective way to the team dynamic. Group sessions help to illustrate how one employee's decision-making can affect the entire team. The free and flexible time that you enjoy in Quadrant Leadership allows you the latitude to use any situation as a platform for employee development.

When you first begin to work in this quadrant, your challenge will be to avoid the temptation to manage. You must stay committed to employee development. In situations where the operation begins to unravel, you must resist every urge to step in and fix it. Addressing the current problem will undoubtedly improve the immediate operations, but it does nothing to change future outcomes. Your goal is to create a team of highly skilled and extremely proficient employees who will be armed with the tools to address any situation.

Keep in mind that many of your employees are coming into Quadrant Leadership very skeptical of the whole process. They will be looking to see if you will keep the promises you made when you introduced the model. Their personal development must be your priority. Your most challenging sessions will occur at the beginning, since old habits sometimes die hard. As you become more comfortable with the model, each session will get better. As you allow yourself to relax and focus on your delivery, you will be able to witness first-hand as extraordinary changes start to take place in your company.

No matter how much your employees improve, there will always be a need for someone to be in charge. For now, the only role that has significantly changed is yours. As far as your managers or charge staff are concerned, it's business as usual. They will continue to be responsible for keeping the operation running smoothly. As your employees begin to accept more personal accountability and take full ownership for their actions, the need for strong supervision significantly diminishes. Eventually, your managers will shift from a hands-on directional style of leadership to being a coordinator of events and activities.

The Art of Coaching

Every employee is told on day one that their priority is to become certified. In the first quadrant, our focus was on skills training. In the second, we introduced less tangible concepts and principles and placed an emphasis on self-initiative attributes. By the time your employees are ready for their first session in the Observer / Coach Quadrant, they have amassed a wealth of information that is about to be tested. It's time for you to implement some effective coaching strategies that will challenge your employees' ability to put the knowledge they have acquired into action.

The art of coaching uses disciplined techniques that require a great deal of practice. Many of these techniques can be difficult to master, and for the majority of us, they do not come naturally. I recommend that before you attempt your first session with an employee in the third quadrant, you do your homework. Make certain that you are comfortable with the subtle but distinct differences between teaching and coaching.

I had the opportunity to hone my coaching skills while working in the training department for McDonald's. I know first-hand how effective coaching can be when done properly. By focusing on the employee's potential rather than a specific standard of excellence, a good coach is able to bring out the best in them.

An experienced coach can make the process look very easy, but I can assure you that it's a skill that takes time to master. There are many great books that discuss good coaching strategies, and I encourage you to do your research before you begin.

As you make your transition into Quadrant Leadership, you are likely to stumble a few times. Never be discouraged by a few sessions that did not turn out quite as you had hoped. Like most things that we eventually become good at, it takes a lot of practice, and with practice comes valuable experience. I'd like to share with you some of the coaching strategies that I found to be highly effective.

Five Game Changing Strategies

1. Use open-ended questions when communicating with your employees 90% of the time.
Answering a question with a question is an effective coaching technique. Your goal in this quadrant is to get the employee to demonstrate independent thinking. Asking nothing but open-ended questions will set that in motion. It will not take long for your employee to realize that you have no intention of providing them with any answers. The time for show-and-tell is over. It's time to call upon what they know and put it into practice.

The most challenging part of this coaching technique is staying with it. Using open-ended questions as your primary form of communication and having it come across as natural and unrehearsed takes a great deal of practice. Try not to sound patronizing or condescending in asking your questions. You want your employee to feel engaged, and your questions should support your belief in their ability to work their way through the situation at hand.

The goal for every employee is to demonstrate that they are ready to be certified. By asking open-ended questions, we validate that they have the knowledge. We then look for them to act upon what they know to make good solid decisions that will ultimately lead to consistent performance at a higher level of proficiency.

While things will be far from perfect in the beginning, each subsequent session in the third quadrant will get progressively better. Your employees will begin to trust in what they have learned, and your job will be to use a variety of effective coaching strategies to draw upon their new found knowledge.

2. Sometimes you must let things get worse before they get better.

For most bosses, this one can be tough to accept. Your natural instinct is to fix problems. The idea of letting something you have already identified as an issue get even worse may not sit well with you. You must look at these situations as learning opportunities that will ultimately make the company stronger. In Quadrant Leadership, we operate in the real world, not an artificial environment. If you are going to let your employee draw upon their resources to find an acceptable solution, then you must resist any temptation to intervene when things get rough. You will be right there at their side offering encouragement and support. No matter how uncomfortable things might feel, you must resist any impulse to direct them towards a solution.

Rely instead on your ability to use effective open-ended questions to point them in the right direction. It may take time to resolve the situation, but as your employee works their way through the process, they begin to find confidence in their abilities. Quadrant Leadership is all about progressive improvement and each time an employee can make a good decision, they are making significant progress.

Some of the development opportunities that have the potential to get even worse involve direct contact with the customer. Even in these situations, you must avoid the temptation to take charge. I suggest you include the customer in the process and share with them what is taking place. Ask for their indulgence and support. If handled properly, the customer feels that some how they have a vested interest in the outcome, and many are happy to play their role. Of course, you always have the option to compensate the customer for a less than favorable experience as a way to thank them for their contribution and to minimize the damage. Either way, your employee is allowed to draw on their resources to work through a real world situation and find an acceptable solution.

3. The secret to successful coaching is extraordinary patience.
In a world driven by deadlines and time commitments, this may be the most valuable coaching strategy of them all. I can only speak for myself, but I found this one to be incredibly difficult to master. The free and flexible time that you have created for yourself has the potential to be tested in a big way during some of these sessions.

Not every one of your employees is going to develop at the same pace. The more complicated a concept is, the more challenging it can be for some employees to process and enact.

I learned this important lesson about the value of patience. If you find yourself in a situation where the employee is struggling, and you are about to pull the plug, remind yourself that you have plenty of time to help them find success, and then carry on. The extra time you invest in this one session may be a critical turning point for the employee. It will become clear to them that you are going beyond what could reasonably be expected.

You will end up garnering a great deal of respect from them. If there was ever a doubt that your commitment to their personal development was genuine, that doubt no longer exists. Experience taught me that many of these employees go on to become some of the best contributors to your company.

Every time I was faced with one of these challenging sessions, I would ask myself two simple questions. Do I believe the employee has the skills and the knowledge to work their way through this problem? Are they putting in a genuine effort? If the answer to both questions was yes, then I owed them my time and attention, and most of all, my patience. I learned first-hand why they say patience is a virtue. I can only tell you that I never considered myself to be a good coach until I learned how to exercise exceptional patience.

4. Take the time to debrief every teachable moment.
Don't let important moments pass without a full review of what has just transpired. While things are still fresh in everyone's mind, talk it through. This is a great opportunity to reinforce the notion that when faced with scenarios where tough decisions are

necessary, there is often more than one solution. It's important to debrief before moving on because these are real-world situations that the employee is likely to encounter again. We can learn as much from a good debriefing session as we did during the actual event. If you have a point you need to drive home, now is the time to do it. Allow your employee the opportunity to share with you what they believe they did well, and where they feel they could have done better. The first step to fixing a problem is to recognize that it exists.

In this quadrant, our most important job is to listen for understanding. If you find yourself doing the majority of the talking, something is wrong. I guarantee that you are no longer asking only open-ended questions. In a coaching session, your job is to ask the question, and then patiently wait for your employee to give you an acceptable answer.

If you jump in too quickly and ask a follow-up question without having the first question answered satisfactorily, you have let the employee off the hook, and they quickly learn that if they simply wait, you will move on. Silence is a powerful tool, so use it wisely.

In the third quadrant, our job is not to critique, inspect, or evaluate. We are there to support our employee as they attempt to draw upon their resources to find viable solutions to real-world problems. While some of our questions can be challenging, they are not meant to frustrate the employee. Using good, open-ended questions will force them to think things through. While we patiently wait for an answer, it is important that our body language and facial expressions reflect a positive demeanor. At no time should we show frustration or appear to be judgmental. No matter how much the employee appears to be struggling, we will do them no favors if we simply spoon-feed them the answer.

By the time your employee is ready for their second session in the third quadrant, they will have a much better idea of what to expect. They will come into the session knowing that they will not be able to rely on you for any of the answers. I guarantee they will put a greater effort in preparing themselves for the session. It will be up to them to demonstrate to you what they are truly capable of.

5. Celebrate progress.

Quadrant Leadership is all about continuous improvement, and it should be celebrated at every opportunity. As long as the accomplishment warrants legitimate praise, it is up to us to make sure that we recognize a job well done. Nothing reinforces repeat behavior better than positive reinforcement. In the next chapter, I will go into praising in more detail. For now, I'll just emphasize that when your employee is able to demonstrate real progress, you should take the opportunity to praise their performance. If it happens to occur in a group setting, then you should encourage every team member to take part in the celebration.

Praising is such a powerful coaching tool requiring two conditions. The first is that the accomplishment warrants the praise. The second is that the employee acted on their own, independent of specific direction from anyone else.

***

These are just a few of the coaching strategies that I have found to be effective for employee development. I suggest that when you first begin to coach, you make a list of any of the strategies you intend to use and keep it close at hand.

Your first few sessions might feel forced and even unnatural because this is not the way you would normally communicate with your employees. Just keep in mind that for your employee to become fully certified, they must be able to make sound decisions without any direct input from you or any member of your team.

By the time your employee is fully certified, they have clearly demonstrated an ability to perform consistently at a high level. This is now the new norm for what will be considered acceptable performance in the future.

Praising Without Conditions

Praising never grows old, no matter how old we grow.

Over time, you will look to many resources to build your library of development material. Never underestimate what you already bring to the table. Your personal experience is an excellent starting point. There is no need to use a lot of fancy language to teach the things you know to be important. Share your personal insight, particularly when it comes to the vision you have for your brand.

The years that I spent working in the training department definitely gave me a solid foundation to work from, but today you have far more resources at your disposal than I ever did. Whether you are looking for information on effective decision-making, team building, time planning, prioritizing, or a host of other topics, all you need do is turn on your computer and start searching. The key is to slowly build your portfolio as you work your way through the model. Use some of your free and flexible time to search for good material that will help you to tap into each employee's full potential.

Until you have conducted a number of sessions in each quadrant, you may want to bring along some notes. Just use them sparingly. The key to a productive one-on-one session is the interaction that takes place between you and your employee. The more you are able to engage them in a healthy exchange of thoughts and ideas, the better the outcome is likely to be.

Over the years, I was constantly on the lookout for good material that could help me in my quest to create a team of highly skilled employees. One source of information was a book written in the 1980s by Ken Blanchard and Spencer Johnson called The One Minute Manager. It is full of great concepts and ideas.

One of my favorite takeaways from The One Minute Manager was the idea of catching people doing things approximately right and praising their effort, rather than waiting for perfection. Many bosses feel that praising a performance that is less than perfect does not make sense. They are concerned that it will send the wrong message to the employee. This is why the most common form of praising used in business is what we call conditional praising.

Let's take a look at a couple of good examples of a conditional praise.

Example 1

"Your smile was genuine, and the customer was impressed, but you forgot to mention the promotion."

Example 2

"You took great initiative, and I can tell that you worked hard on this. If only you had asked me about the color scheme first, you could have avoided so many problems."

Employees who are routinely treated to conditional praising will tell you that they do not have a positive view of this kind of communication. They know that any good feeling they get from the first part of your comments will quickly be replaced with what they did wrong, or something they need to improve.

Legitimate praising has no conditions attached. The objective of praising is to allow the employee to feel good about themselves and enjoy a sense of pride in a job well done. It should be given time to manifest, and the employee should be able to experience the feelings that come from being genuinely appreciated.

In Quadrant Leadership, our objective is to take the condition right out of the praise. To accomplish this, we need to adjust the approach we take. It takes a little getting used to because you have to catch yourself before you deliver the condition. Once you see how much you can accomplish by making this simple change, my hope is that you will abandon conditional praising altogether.

The first step is to legitimize the praise by letting it stand on its own. To do this, we sever the conditional praise in half and separate the two components by time and circumstance. Let me clarify what I mean by using the same two examples as before.

> *"You have a great smile, and the customer was impressed with the way you presented yourself. It is that kind of service that sets us apart from our competitors. Great effort!"*

Here you allow the employee time to experience that feel-good sensation that comes with positive recognition. Praising can be the least expensive, yet most effective way to raise an employee's performance level. Recognizing their positive behavior, ensures that it will be repeated. This is such an important tool, yet most of the time the benefit is lost when the positive comment is immediately squashed by criticism in the form of a conditional praise.

The key to finding success with this approach is to make sure that there is a clear break between the actual praise and what needs to be improved upon. The easiest way to accomplish this is to change the subject entirely. We need to have a healthy separation between the two parts of the conditional praise.

Each situation will be a little different, but you will sense when the time is right to address other matters such as the importance of customers knowing about current promotions. Your employee will still be feeling the positive halo effect of the praise and is likely to be far more receptive to your feedback. Your goal should be to have them make the connection between what they did well, and what would have made it even better. You can accomplish this without the need to criticize the missed opportunity.

The exchange should end with your employee making a commitment to inform all their customers about current promotions. If you are able to make this important adjustment to the way you approach these types of situations, you will have successfully addressed the issue at hand, and your employee will leave the exchange with their positive mindset still intact.

> *"You took great initiative, and I can see that you put in a lot of hard work on this. I am really impressed. Great job!"*

Praise must always be legitimate and warranted. It is all relative to where each employee is in their development. What can be a big deal for one employee may be nothing more than routine for another.

In the second example, we take the same approach and make sure that we have a clean break from the behavior that earned the praise and the behavior that needs to be corrected. After an adequate amount of time has passed, you can now address the area of opportunity.

> *"I noticed that you changed the color scheme on the project. Do you feel it will create any challenges for the rest of the team?"*

The praise you bestowed upon them earlier was indeed legitimate and well-deserved, but clearly they made an error in not considering their choice of color. The positive mindset they are operating out of should make them far more receptive to your question. The key is to get the employee to recognize the error on their own, and take responsibility for the fact that their decision has created other problems. Your comments should focus on the issue rather than calling into question the employee's decision-making skills.

> *"When you are preparing to do a big project like this can you see how important it is that you have all the information you need before you proceed?"*

Sometimes a boss has nothing good to say at all and still tries to use a conditional praise to soften the blow. The problem is that the praise is so disingenuous that it has no credibility, making the situation even worse. In a case like this, you are better off simply to address the issue at hand and get it over with, rather than trying to sugarcoat it with false praise.

Whether you make the decision to transition to Quadrant Leadership or not, you should seriously consider getting rid of conditional praising. I am convinced that if you make the effort, you will soon realize the benefits that can be derived from this simple technique. It will lead to a lot more stand alone praising, which could prove to be a challenge for some. It really depends on how you view praising in general.

Some bosses believe that too much praising leads to complacency. In all of the years that I worked in the Quadrant Leadership Model, I never found this to be true. It is a simple fact that people who work in a positive environment are more inclined to give more of themselves than those who feel their effort is never appreciated.

The Search for a More Efficient Company

When I first set out to implement Quadrant Leadership, I was prepared to let the chips fall where they may. The time had come to abandon a playbook that was decades old. I knew it would repeat in the back of my mind, like a familiar soundtrack set to auto loop. If I were to be successful, I had to find the discipline to stay committed to the principles of the model.

Looming large was the reality of my illness. The need to create an extraordinary team, capable of handling virtually any situation in my absence, was all the motivation I needed. I was totally convinced that the theory behind Quadrant Leadership was rock solid as long as I was prepared to stick with it.

Those early days were all about trial and error. If I tried something that didn't work the way I hoped it would, I refused to let it get to me. It was all just part of the learning curve, and I had to accept the fact that effort alone was not going to get me the results I needed. Rather than becoming discouraged, I would simply change my strategy and begin again. The model is forgiving that way, and so are your employees. If they believe that you have their best interest at heart, they will cut you some slack. I know it sounds corny, but once they sense your commitment to their personal development, even your biggest critics will start to come around and begin to appreciate your efforts.

One of the important lessons I learned early on was never to try to anticipate how any particular session might turn out. Some of the sessions I prepared long and hard for fell short of the mark.

Others that began with a simple agenda turned out to be incredibly productive, both to my surprise and delight.

I have already warned you of the dangers of turning the model into some gigantic administrative beast. There's no need for it. This is a philosophy of leadership that you will come to live and breathe every single day. Creating individual files and documenting detailed progress may seem important, but it will take you away from where you should really be spending your time. Your greatest returns will occur in the here and now, working with your employees as they tackle real-world situations.

Learn to listen to your instincts, and be prepared to change your strategy at a moment's notice. The model will give you the flexibility to go to whatever quadrant makes the most sense for the development opportunity you are dealing with. If you try something and it doesn't work, just accept it and move on. Many successful sessions will give you the confidence and the motivation to look for alternative strategies that will address some of your more challenging development opportunities.

The more you work in the model, the more comfortable you will become. Your demeanor is a huge part of setting the temperament for a productive session. If things are frantic and chaotic, that tense atmosphere will have a direct effect on the outcome. Set the example by appearing relaxed and un-rushed. I admit that this can be a tall order, particularly when the business is not running well. Your instinct will be to step in and get things back on track. If you do that, you will miss a huge development opportunity that your employees could have significantly benefited from. When faced with situations like this, you must stay true to your purpose. After all, this is the real world, and your employees are likely to be presented with similar situations in the future.

Take full advantage of what is happening, and coach your employees to draw on their resources. Make them believe that they are more than capable of playing their role in finding viable solutions. Remain calm and exercise extreme patience. It is important to understand that these are exactly the kinds of situations that will validate your employees' ability to use the knowledge they have acquired. Every time one of your employees has a successful session, you move one step closer to amassing that army of highly proficient problem solvers bent on protecting the core values of your brand.

With every full certification that an employee earns, your operation grows more efficient. A team that is well connected is a formidable force. Productivity is an important component in the efficiency equation, but there are other aspects as well. The free and flexible time that the model gives you has many benefits. Because your focus is no longer on running the day-to-day operations, you become more aware of the intricate details of your business.

I found myself looking for redundancy and duplication at every turn. The more time you spend in the Observer / Coach Quadrant, the more opportunity you have to evaluate every aspect of your operation. Questioning whether something is necessary has nothing to do with a lack of faith in the way that things are done. If anything, it reaffirms that the majority of your business practices fully support your core initiatives. For me, it was all about improving efficiency.

These things are more likely to be functional aspects of the business rather than employee performance opportunities. I began by reviewing every job description. I wanted to be sure that every task and job function had a purpose that was still relevant. Did they meet the current needs of the business? Was there redundancy from one job to the next? Eliminating duplication had the potential to save time and resources and improve efficiency.

I questioned every administrative duty to see if they were necessary. I might have given you the impression that I am anti-administration, but I can assure you that I am fully aware of the importance of maintaining sound business practices. It just seems that many businesses today have become carried away with paperwork.

I remember attending a seminar in the early eighties on the role computers would play in our future. The fellow delivering the lecture made the prediction that the need to keep a paper copy of anything would be unnecessary within ten years. He surmised that the office of the future would be entirely paperless. In this new world, data would be stored on something called floppy discs, the early predecessor to hard drives and cloud technology. I don't have to tell you that his prediction was a little off. Paper consumption in business today is higher than it has ever been. Perhaps people feel the need to have a copy of something "just in case." Maybe it's a genuine fear that important data will simply vanish in the vacuum of cyberspace. Or maybe it's just the sheer volume of information available today, courtesy of the digital world. If you think about it, based on his prediction, photocopiers and printers should no longer even exist. Instead, there are more of them than ever spewing out reams of paperwork. In some companies they're even working overtime.

***

In your quest to improve your business, you will begin to take a closer look at your entire physical plant. Is there a better configuration? Is your business being presented in the best possible light? Sometimes simple changes to your physical plant can make a significant difference to the customer's perception of your business. Use your free and flexible time to talk to your customers on a regular basis. Having the ability to view your business through the eyes of the consumer is critical to maintaining long-term brand loyalty. No business, no matter how successful it is, can afford to rest on its laurels.

Depending on the nature of your business, you might also consider repositioning your employees. In the spirit of team synergy, it might make sense to switch offices or bring desks closer together to improve communication and interaction. If you have employees working in the field who rely on office personnel, it is important to get input from both parties to identify any barriers that are inhibiting their ability to do a good job. Quadrant Leadership has already changed the working relationship between you and your employees. Use your one-on-one sessions to gather feedback on these important issues.

Your goal is to eliminate any barrier that prevents your employees from doing their job well. Let's be clear here: change for change's sake is a complete waste of time and resources. If, however, the change will improve your business in a meaningful way, and it helps your employees do a better job, then it should be implemented as soon as possible.

Many of these changes are minor, but occasionally you will stumble upon something that will lead you to consider a major shift. I have a good example that took place in my own business.

Before I begin my story, let me make this critical observation. It has been my experience that a paradigm can be a tough nut to crack, particularly when we're talking about big corporations. When something has been done a certain way for a long time, it can be an uphill battle to convince the powers that be that it should change. Paradigms have nothing to do with what is best, or cost effective, or even the most efficient. They just happen to be the way something has always been done for as long as anyone can remember. For most people, that is reason enough to let sleeping dogs lie. I was about to find out just how true that statement is.

The last day of the month is a very busy day in a McDonald's restaurant. For many companies, there are a number of additional administrative duties that must be completed as part of the month-end process. For a McDonald's manager, the most time-consuming of these tasks is the completion of a full food and paper inventory. Over the years, as more products have been added to the menu, the challenge of keeping track of all of these items has grown exponentially. In Business and the Bottom Line, we talked about the importance of optimizing every variable cost that affects the bottom line. For a McDonald's restaurant, the single biggest variable expense on the profit and loss statement is the food cost percentage.

It's important that the inventory is accurately counted and then calculated since the final number has a significant impact on the bottom line. Managers who are scheduled to work a month-end night shift must balance their time between managing their night shift operations and completing as many pre-month-end duties as possible.

Sales for the last day of the month are typically higher than the norm, and can be even higher if month-end happens to fall on a payday or a busier day of the week such as a Friday. Higher volume restaurants will often schedule two managers to close on a month-end night to share the extra workload, but for many McDonald's restaurants, the month-end is completed by the closing manager.

When I was the head of the training department, I used a line every time I addressed a group of new assistant managers attending their first class in our training facility. I would remind them that *'floor control is not a part-time job.'* The term 'floor control' in McDonald's relates to managing the customer experience. Over the course of the week, I would repeat that statement many times. Floor control is the single most important job responsibility of any McDonald's manager. As Ray Kroc would say, "Nothing is more important than QSC." As far as Ray was concerned, having the ability to deliver outstanding quality, service, and cleanliness on a consistent basis mattered more than anything else, including month end duties. The fact that my managers stayed on the floor and made sure the customers were taken care of demonstrated their commitment to floor control.

That evening, we were not able to do a single bit of month-end pre-close. When the last customer was finally served, we took a much-needed break before preparing to tackle the month-end duties. It could have been a long night for my managers, but I decided to stay and lend a hand with the inventory count. This number is so important to the profit and loss statement that accuracy is paramount.

The time I was spending in the Observer / Coach Quadrant had me taking a long look at every aspect of the business. That evening, I added month-end to the list. It just seemed to me that there should be a better way. After a week of tossing various ideas around, I finally felt that I had come up with a viable solution that I believed was an excellent alternative. The only catch was that it would challenge a paradigm that had been in place from the beginning.

For McDonald's, the term 'month-end' is taken literally to mean the last minute of the last hour of the last day of the month. My solution was to designate two p.m. as closing time on the final day of the month. As I saw it, there were many pros to moving month-end into the day shift.

The first two advantages were a fresh mind and more people resources. In most McDonald's restaurants, there are usually more employees working the day shift who could lend a hand. There would be no need for any pre-closing duties since the inventory and the ledgers could be completed without any interruption. The night shift manager could focus on floor control and running an excellent shift without the challenge of preparing for a month-end. Once all the calculations were completed, there would be ample time to fix any obvious errors and immediately recheck inventory counts if necessary. The chance that fatigue would play a factor in the accuracy of numbers was virtually eliminated.

The whole thing made so much sense to me, and so when the next month-end rolled around, I put my plan into action. We pulled the closing sales report at two p.m. and although we remained open, from an accounting perspective we were effectively closed for the day.

Our reporting obligations each month required that we submit monthly gross sales and total customer counts to the corporate office. By pulling the closing sales report early, we would be ten hours short in our tally. Those sales, of course, were not lost. They would simply be added to the following month's totals when the closing report would once again be pulled at two p.m. From that point on, the sales for every month would be comparable. We would be reporting the same amount of operating hours as every other McDonald's. The only difference would be the start and finish times.

My managers loved the change. By the time most McDonald's were preparing to go into their dinner hour, we would have our month-end completed. My managers could turn their full attention to managing the business, knowing that their month-end obligation had been met in full. We still waited until closing time to report our numbers, but that was merely a formality.

A few months later, after everything was flowing smoothly, I informed my corporate counterparts of the changes that I had made. To say that they were unimpressed would be putting it mildly. When I asked them what the issue was, the only answer they could come up with was that every restaurant was required to follow the same procedures, without exception. I reminded them that I had worked at our Thurlow Street location back in the late seventies. This restaurant was located in the business district of downtown Vancouver, and city bylaws at the time did not permit us to be open on Sundays. Over the years, we had a number of month-ends in that location that were completed a full day ahead of every other restaurant in the city. Despite the fact that a precedent had already been set many years earlier, the resistance I faced was a classic example of the power of a paradigm.

I had given them a list of reasons why this was a positive change that would protect restaurant operations, improve month-end accuracy and efficiency, and raise management morale. Many years later when I sold my restaurants, month-end duties changed back to the closing hour and once again, the universe was aligned.

For me, there is great irony in the fact that many present-day McDonald's restaurants operate on a twenty-four-hour clock. From my perspective, the traditional closing time holds even less importance than it did before. The resistance I encountered was a mindset issue and nothing more. When you think that nothing was lost and yet so much could be gained from making this simple change, it makes you wonder how many more paradigms are out there standing in the way of real progress and a far more efficient way of doing business.

Team Thinking First

So far, my primary focus has been on conducting individual employee sessions. Most companies require the collaborative effort of many employees to meet the expectations of their customers. How much or how little your employees are dependent on one another will have a lot to do with the nature of your business. One of the things that makes the Quadrant Leadership Model such a powerful development tools is how well it works in a group setting.

Whether you are conducting a skills training exercise in the first quadrant, introducing a brand new set of employees to the *Universal Truths of Employment* in the second, or assessing team synergy in the third, the model has the ability to take on the development needs of virtually any size group. Team Thinking First is an exercise that takes place many times over in the third quadrant. The objective of these sessions is always the same. You are continually assessing the team's ability to apply advanced self-initiative attributes effectively.

Similar to the basic attributes, the advanced initiatives focus on the employee's role in the team dynamic. Remember that this is merely a base template that you are encouraged to expand upon to meet the needs of your business.

Advance Self-Initiative Attributes

Team Accountability - A willingness to look at the bigger picture and share responsibility for the actions of the entire team. This includes sharing accountability for decisions made collectively, or by other employees on behalf of the team.

Scope of Work - Communicating, connecting and coordinating the individual roles of each employee to come together as one unit. Utilizing team synergy to do everything within the power of the group to meet or exceed customer expectations. Through experience and knowledge, each employee demonstrates a willingness to accept the responsibilities of the team as their own.

Short-Term Decision Making - Making critical decisions that directly affect the performance of the team in a positive way.

Long-Term Decision Making - Anticipating potential issues and barriers based on experience and knowledge. Implementing long-term solutions through collective team input to address recurring issues.

Multi-Tasking - Setting the example by looking for every opportunity to coordinate tasks with other members of your team.

Time Planning and Prioritizing - Effective use of time management to prioritize specific elements of your job that strengthen the efficiency of the team.

Personal Work Ethic - Rising to the level of intensity necessary to support team initiatives. A willingness to take on more responsibility for group decisions for the entire operation to function at a higher level.

Team Thinking First is all about placing the best interests of the team ahead of self-interests.

Beginning in the second quadrant and carrying over into the third, we spend a great deal of time exploring behaviors common to well-connected, highly functional teams. What makes them so different from every other team? What does it mean to be a part of a team that has achieved this status? What role do leaders play within a team dynamic of this nature? Does a highly proficient team even need a traditional leader?

These and many other questions are addressed as your employees examine the fundamentals that are required to take a team to the next level. One of the most important lessons that you hope every employee will take away from working in a highly productive team environment is that really good leaders have an ability to recognize when their talents are required to lead the charge and when they are better suited to a supporting role.

Highly competitive people tend to struggle with the concept of team equality. The idea of having to take direction from one of their peers does not sit well with those who need to prove that they are better than others. They tend to gravitate towards self-interests, often missing the point behind team synergy. They define success by what they bring to the table and are far more comfortable in a competitive environment where being the best confirms that they have proven their self-worth.

Team Thinking First sessions are specifically designed to demonstrate how much stronger a unified, well-connected team is than a group of individuals serving self-interests. Most leaders who have enjoyed a long and successful career will tell you that the real secret lies in having the ability to get the most you possibly can out of every person you are working with. The positive character attributes that these leaders display plays a critical role in their ability to develop a winning team.

Dominant personalities who fail to learn these important lessons often go on to become competent micro-managers. Their need to stay in control of every situation in order to manage the outcome means they miss a tremendous opportunity to see what team synergy is capable of delivering. Team synergy works because we take advantage of every bit of talent at our disposal. The role the entire team plays in making it to the championship game is just as important as the guy who scores the winning goal. To function at the top of their game, each member of the team must be prepared to set aside personal self-serving interests in favor of doing their part for the greater good.

Through the many team exercises you will put your employees through, the objective is to get them to embrace their advance self-initiative attributes. By placing team interests ahead of self-interest, they are demonstrating specific qualities that are found in successful leaders. To lead a winning team, you must first understand what makes one work. The way they conduct themselves within the group dynamic demonstrates a level of understanding that is an essential ingredient in creating a winning team.

From your perspective, the more time you can spend in group sessions, the more opportunities there will be to practice the use of advanced self-initiative attributes. Creating teams that function at this level takes extraordinary patience and a whole lot of practice. It may take some time, but in the end, it will be well worth the effort.

Even alpha-type personalities cannot ignore the benefits of being a part of a highly proficient team that takes full advantage of the entire pool of talent. High functioning teams are a thing of beauty. The vibe they give off is infectious, and it has the ability to motivate others to join the club. I cannot predict when this will happen for you, given that there is no fixed time schedule for the progress that your employees will make within the model. What I can tell you is this: when it does happen, you will have reached a significant milestone in your quest to create extraordinary brand identity.

Quadrant Four
The Mentor / Advisor

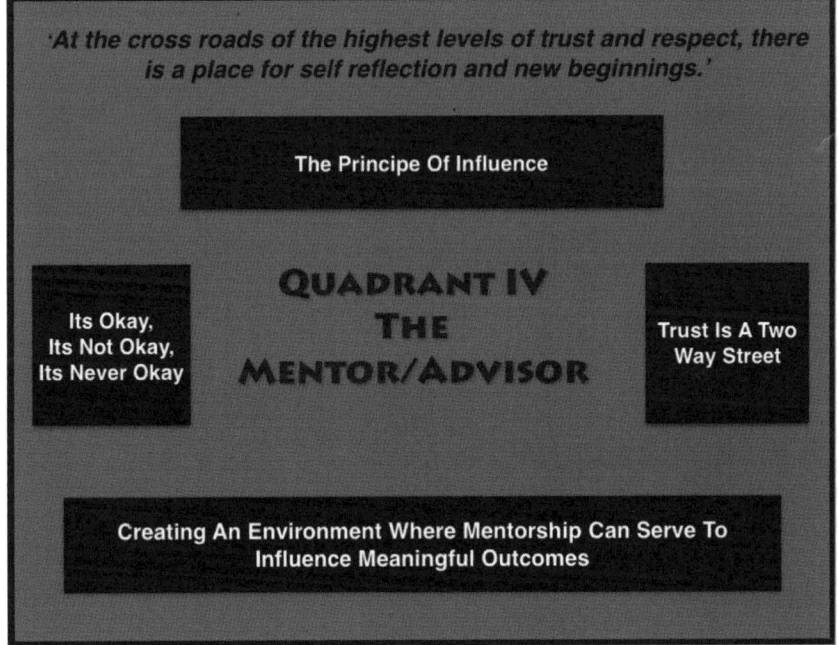

There is a significant difference between possessing a competitive will to win, and the need to win at all costs.

The Principle of Influence

Change is seldom easy, sometimes disruptive, and often hard to accept. For most of us, it is in our nature to resist change. We tend to be creatures of habit and routine, enjoying a certain comfort level in knowing what lies ahead. Most people are highly suspicious when it comes to change, particularly if they believe it to be unnecessary. What's the motivation behind the change? Whose decision was it? Is it really going to make a difference? While most of us are prepared to accept that some change is inevitable, too much, too quickly, can be disastrous.

There are many ways to enact change. Governments legislate it; companies impose it, and both see it as their right to do so. Change can result from circumstances outside of anyone's control, such as a natural disaster that wipes out a way of life, or a downturn in the economy that results in job losses and business closures. For most people, the word change can be unsettling.

While change is indeed inevitable, buy-in is not. Governments, of course, have the right to impose penalties and fines for failing to adhere to new rules and regulations, and companies can invoke any number of consequences on employees who fail to follow changes in policies and procedures. While enforcement may work to varying degrees, it's hardly the answer.

Businesses are required to make changes all the time, and it is certainly their prerogative to do so. Whether to streamline operations to protect the bottom line, or to improve the overall customer experience, the need for change to stay one step ahead of the competition will always be necessary. The key is to be able to implement change that is embraced by your employees rather than forced upon them. How do you accomplish such a feat? The answer lies in your ability to influence the way your employees deal with change.

One of the many reasons why the Quadrant Leadership Model is such an effective development tool is that it fully subscribes to the Principle of Influence. By definition, Influence is the capacity or power to have an effect on someone else. Influence is a powerful attribute that can be used for good and evil. The principle of influence is based on a well-established and proven formula that is stated as follows:

> **Respect x Trust = Influence**. When both of these important character attributes are in place, the sphere of influence can be significant.

The Quadrant Leadership Model rests on a foundation of mutual respect. In the second quadrant, we talk about the positive character attributes that are common to successful people. Most people who are admired for their accomplishments are also highly respected. For many of these people, the respect they have earned is equal to, or greater than, all of their achievements.

While we spend little time discussing negative character attributes in Quadrant Leadership, we make it clear that showing disrespect for another employee is simply unacceptable. Our objective in the second quadrant is to focus on the positive attributes that will help our employees achieve their goals. At the top of that list is earning the respect of the people they work with.

It's important that your employees can distinguish the difference between being respected and being liked. While it would be nice for both to exist, a working relationship is not a popularity contest. Using common courtesy, engaging in meaningful dialog that includes eye contact and active listening skills, as well as demonstrating team thinking first, are all excellent examples of showing respect for your fellow employee. If two people do not socialize with each other outside of work, that is their choice. What matters is the way they conduct themselves while representing your company.

Early on, we teach the importance of climbing the trust ladder. Trust plays such an important role when it comes to earning independence. Your employees know that if they want to be granted the freedom to make decisions on their own without the need for direct supervision, then they must earn your trust as well as that of your managers. In Quadrant Leadership, we spend a great deal of time emphasizing the importance of earning both trust and respect. The most important thing we can do is walk the talk every day. The way we conduct ourselves within the model will play a critical role in our ability to influence future outcomes. As the majority of your employees successfully earn their first full certification, the sphere of influence you now enjoy will grant you extraordinary access to a rich resource of potential as they eagerly await their next challenge.

A Matter of Trust

While the Mentor Quadrant has the potential to contribute a great deal to the ongoing development of your employees, it will not be for everyone. The parameters that define the mentor relationship are specific and unforgiving. Any attempt to implement the fourth quadrant without the proper elements in place will fail.

The dictionary defines a mentor as an experienced and trusted advisor. While the level of experience you bring to the table is important, it makes no difference what position you hold in your company. The catalyst that cements the mentor relationship is the level of trust that exists between you and your employee. The idea that we choose to mentor is at best an illusion. Despite any declaration on our part, the level of mentorship that you will achieve will be chosen for you by those who actively seek out your guidance.

When I first set out to implement the Quadrant Leadership Model, I devoted the majority of my time to the certification process. I knew that I would have to earn my credentials before I could ever consider introducing the Mentor Quadrant into the development process. One of the most difficult things for me to accept was that despite my best effort to earn every employee's trust, it did not happen. The reasons were as varied as the circumstances. If a relationship has been compromised prior to your transition into Quadrant Leadership, the feelings that linger are likely to carry over, making it virtually impossible to wipe the slate entirely clean.

Some of the employees who are clearly under-performing will forfeit the opportunity to start over and will remain highly skeptical of your motives. You will also encounter employees who have trust issues that have nothing to do with anyone in particular.

They simply cannot bring themselves to place the kind of trust in anyone that would open the doors for them to participate in the Mentor Quadrant.

No matter the reasons, any attempt on your part to force the issue would be a mistake. Your only true recourse is to keep the lines of communication open and make sure that every employee knows that you are always available to talk.

I should point out that not every employee requires the kind of additional support that the fourth quadrant can provide. Some of your employees will do just fine without it. Your relationship with them is likely already on solid ground. If they feel the need for some advice, they will have no problem seeking you out.

Try to avoid over-thinking the Mentor Quadrant. If you allow your relationships to progress in a natural way and stay committed to the four principle strategies that drive the philosophy behind Quadrant Leadership, you will have no trouble earning the kind of trust and respect that will open the doors to the fourth quadrant. Let's look at these strategies from the perspective of building trust.

Strategy 1. (The Development Roadmap)

Establish the Quadrant Leadership Model as the preeminent tool for employee development. Ensure that the quality of execution and the caliber of material substantially raises employee performance.

Nothing builds credibility faster than impressive results. By fully engaging the Quadrant Leadership Model, you are providing your employees with the kind of personal development that will substantially improve their odds for success. Every underperformer that you are able to turn around will be a major boost to your credibility. Consider each of your one-on-one sessions as an opportunity to improve your relationship. You will find that if you let things evolve at their own pace, the Mentor Quadrant will become a natural part of the development process.

Once you establish your rhythm and learn to relax, your employees will too, and they will begin to enjoy the time you spend together. Demeanor is so important because it sets the tone for the session. Having the ability to put people at ease can be a critical first step toward fully engaging the learning process.

Finally, if you are able to avoid falling back into old management habits every time something goes wrong, your employees will learn to trust you when you say that their personal development is truly your top priority.

Strategy 2. (A Clear Understanding)

Commit to creating healthy working partnerships that are based on mutual respect and reciprocal trust.

The word 'partnership' suggests a mutual understanding that we are in this together. In every good partnership, there is an element of give and take. Both parties expect the other to bring something of value to the table. In Quadrant Leadership, the value you bring is your promise to provide every employee with the highest caliber of ongoing personal development you can. In return, you fully expect that they will be prepared to take full accountability for the decisions they make, and for the decisions that are made as part of a collective team.

This is an important discussion that must take place early in the relationship. Your employees must recognize that trust is a two-way street. As hard as you are working to earn their trust, they must also be making the same effort to earn yours. If they hope to enjoy the freedom that comes with working independent of direct supervision, then they must first earn the privilege. There must be no doubt as to what each party expects from the other.

It is this understanding against which all future progress will be measured. As your employee continues to develop and take on new responsibilities, there is a clear expectation that the level of accountability will grow exponentially.

Strategy 3. (The Validation Platform)

Invoke a strong sense of ownership and accountability by coaching potential that builds both confidence and personal commitment.

The third quadrant is where all of the hard work really begins. Your role is to challenge your employees to put into practice everything that the have been taught. The time for show and tell is over, and while your coaching strategies will sometimes push the boundaries of emotion from frustration to elation, your top priority will be to make sure that your employee has all of the knowledge and skills they require to be extremely successful in your company. The sense of pride they will experience when they have proven their ability to make significant contributions to your business will strengthen your relationship and make the path to the Mentor Quadrant a natural progression.

Strategy 4. (Everyone is Welcome)

Create an environment in which open and honest communication free of judgment and criticism can lead to meaningful change.

A great deal of the dialogue that takes place in the Mentor Quadrant is extremely personal. Your employee will be holding you to the strictest of confidence. Your role in this quadrant is first to listen for understanding and then offer valuable insight. Despite the challenges associated with self-inflicted inappropriate behavior, your employee will be counting on you not to give up on them. For you to make progress in this quadrant, they must believe that you are their advocate and not their adversary.

Always remember that your employee must initiate the Mentor Quadrant. Until that time comes, take every opportunity to let them know that the door is always open. Use your one-on-one sessions as an opportunity to ask them if there is anything else they would like to talk about. Remain calm and relaxed and allow them as much time as they need to reflect. If the climate is right, they will begin to talk, and the door to the Mentor Quadrant will open.

I must caution that you need to decide early on in the process whether you intend to restrict the mentor relationship to workplace issues. If you open up the dialogue to any topic, you must be prepared to accept the fact that your counsel may be sought on issues of a far more personal nature. For me, this was never a problem, but some may feel that this takes things too far. In the end, only you can decide. Whatever discussions you engage in, you will be expected to keep their confidence. I can see no circumstance short of an illegal act or imminent danger where it would be acceptable to break that confidence. If you ever do, you will never regain their trust and your reputation with other employees could be severely compromised.

This is such an important quadrant because it offers a way to confront some of the most challenging performance issues, free of conflict and confrontation. In any other environment, addressing matters of a personal nature often puts the employee on the defensive, and the lines of communication tend to shut down completely.

In the Mentor Quadrant, your employee is looking for help, not criticism. By removing contentious issues from the public eye and addressing them in a private setting, free of judgment, there is a good chance that they can be resolved. Some of the most challenging issues that we have to deal with involve inappropriate behavior. My experience has been that ignoring or marginalizing conduct that negatively affects other employees will come back to haunt you in a big way. Our goal in the Mentor Quadrant is to address these types of issues long before they have an opportunity to manifest into something far more damaging. Perhaps the most valuable aspect of the Mentor Quadrant is that it gives you a legitimate platform to deal effectively with highly contentious issues and find viable solutions.

It's Okay, It's Not Okay, It's Never Okay

Every company, regardless of the service or product they provide, is in the business of people. Despite our best efforts to promote mutual respect and reinforce the benefits of positive character attributes, a highly competitive work environment is often a place for conflict to occur. Opposing opinions, strong personalities, tight timelines, and a breakdown in communication can all lead to some form of confrontation. Minor skirmishes tend to have a short shelf life and work themselves out on their own. Altercations of a more serious nature, however, can have significant consequences.

One of the things I loved most about Quadrant Leadership is what it taught me about the importance of self awareness. Once I committed myself to the Mentor Quadrant, I completely changed the way I approached issues pertaining to inappropriate behavior. Conflict resolution is such an important skill for every boss to master. The more time you can spend in the fourth quadrant, the more you begin to understand human nature better. Digging deeper into what drives inappropriate behavior became a critical first step in addressing poor people practices.

The real strength of the Mentor Quadrant is the dialog itself. Once you are successful in creating an environment in which your employees feel free to express their true feelings free from judgment and criticism, they will begin to open up and offer you some extraordinary insight. The more discussions I participated in that dealt specifically with behavioral issues, the more I began to recognize an emerging pattern. My observations lead me to conclude that most of these issues could be traced to one of two sources.

The first source is what I refer to as **Learned** or **Environmental Behavior**. This is behavior that is rooted in a core set of beliefs, many of which are formed early on. These types of beliefs continue to manifest throughout our entire lives. They are often born from personal experience, and are largely influenced by the environment we live in and the people we most closely associate with. We include tolerated behavior in this group as well. Even if we cannot identify the specific source, the fact that the behavior is allowed to continue even when deemed inappropriate suggests that it will surface as a behavioral issue down the road.

Let's look at some of the most common behaviors that fall into this category and the four-step action plan that can be effective in dealing with them.

Learned or Environmental Behavior That Can Lead to Conflict

- disrespect
- impatience
- rudeness
- condescension
- sarcasm
- arrogance / judgemental tendencies
- trust issues
- prejudicial tendencies
- bullying / intimidation tactics

Four-Step Action Plan

Step One
Recognize the Degree of Impropriety

Each behavior will fall into one of three categories.

It's Okay
It can be frustrating when an employee has worked hard on a task only to be let down by someone else. While it's certainly their prerogative to express disappointment and hold the other person accountable, it is not acceptable to call the other employee's character into question. Accusing someone of being lazy or incompetent or any other attack on their personal character changes the situation from something that is entirely appropriate to something that is not. Having the ability to express frustration and disappointment without making it personal requires a clear understanding of the kind of behavior that protects relationships and the kind that creates conflict. By voicing their disappointment with the result rather than attacking the other person's character your employee will be able to make their point while maintaining the integrity of the relationship. This skill will serve them well in the future.

It's Not Okay
This is inappropriate behavior that has the potential to cause cumulative damage. While one or two isolated incidents of rudeness are not likely to do significant harm, repeated offenses will create serious issues for the employee. They run the risk of losing the respect of their peer group, and the ability to influence outcomes. Behavior that frequently involves sarcasm or indifference towards others will earn the employee a reputation as someone who possesses poor people skills. Unless the employee can clearly see the damage that this kind of behavior is doing to their credibility, they will make no effort to change.

It's Never Okay
The word never is about as definitive as you can get. The damage that can be done by behavior that falls into this category is often irreversible. It's vital that the employee recognizes the gravity of the situation. Repeating this kind of behavior can have far-reaching implications. There is no room for bullying or intimidation tactics in a credible company. I say credible because some companies promote these tactics to achieve results. Acts of sexism, racism, or any other form of prejudice are not only unacceptable, they can also be grounds for immediate termination. There is no circumstance that will justify this behavior.

Step Two
Find the Source of the Learned Behavior

The second step is to trace the learned behavior back to its point of origin. Keep in mind that if the behavior is based on a belief system that is still practiced in the home, it will be difficult to reverse without the employee being prepared to abandon a familiar way of thinking. Finding the source may involve some major prompting on your part. The employee may be reluctant to admit that they learned it from someone they respect. It might simply be something that has been tolerated by the people in their sphere of influence for a long time, even though it is highly inappropriate.

Step Three
Debunk the Thinking the Behavior Is Based Upon

Before a new way of thinking can be embraced, the employee must be able to recognize the flawed thinking that allowed the old behavior to exist in the first place. Unless they genuinely see the error in their thinking, there is little chance that they will change the way they act or what they believe.

I should point out that your success throughout this process will depend entirely on the level of respect and trust that exits between you and the employee. If they truly believe that you have their best interest at heart, they will make a concerted effort to recognize the flawed thinking. These discussions are often candid and to the point. Your relationship will allow for this kind of exchange. There is no sense sugar coating something that must be addressed before any meaningful change can take place.

Step Four
Walk the Talk

When inappropriate behavioral issues arise, the damage can often be difficult to reverse. Just because the employee claims to have changed their ways, does not mean everyone is prepared to believe them. This can be frustrating for the offender, who is trying hard to turn the page. While you encourage them to continue to rebuild these relationships, they need to remember that they have only themselves to blame for their predicament. You may have to remind them a few times that it is going to take time, patience, and a genuine desire on their part to earn back their lost credibility.

***

The second source of behavioral issues is **Character-Driven Behavior**. The human psyche is a complex beast made up of many different character elements that are deeply entrenched in our DNA. While many parts of our personality can bring out our best qualities, most people are willing to admit to at least a few character flaws. A person who possesses a hair-trigger temper, for instance, will tell you that they are not proud of it, but no amount of wishing on their part will make it disappear. A person who has jealous tendencies cannot tell you why they have them, but they are aware that they have the potential to influence their behavior.

Identifying which type of behavior we are dealing with is an important first step in determining how we approach the solution. We need to be able to identify the types of inappropriate behavior that can actually be changed and the types that can only be managed. Many learned or environmental behaviors are rooted in a strong set of core beliefs. If we are able to debunk the thinking that the belief is based upon, then there is an excellent chance that the behavior can be reversed.

When it comes to inappropriate behavior attributed to an employee's character, the only true course of action is to manage it. The notion that we can somehow change who someone is on the inside is foolhardy. Insisting the employee just stop the behavior is hardly a solution. The action plan that will address character driven behavior focuses on the danger of the conduct and the most effective ways to manage it. Character driven behaviors tend to be far more complex than learned behaviors and most often fall into one of three subcategories.

Character Driven Behavior That Can Lead to Conflict

Ethical Behavior
A need to win no matter the cost or collateral damage
Personal word is suspect / credibility issues / prepared to compromise confidentiality if it means you will win
Issues of morality and conscience such as honesty and integrity
A question of the truth. No problem lying for self preservation

Self Preservation Behavior
Control Issues - Micro Manager Tendencies
Sharing Issues
Selfishness

> ## Character Driven Behavior That Can Lead to Conflict
>
> **Emotional Behavior**
> Anger / rage / temper
> Jealousy
> A need for revenge / spiteful / vindictive tendencies
> Easily annoyed / little or no compassion / lack of patience
> Operate from extreme sides of the emotion scale. It is either love or hate, for or against, no in between. You are either my friend or enemy
> Inability to forgive. Hold grudges
> Pessimistic perspective. Predominantly negative personality.

While some of these could be considered learned behaviors, the test is whether you believe that the behavior can be permanently reversed or whether it is more likely that it needs to be managed.

The four-step action plan for Character-Driven Behavior differs from the Learned Behavior action plan because the driver is the employee themselves.

***

Four Step Action Plan

Step One
Recognize the Degree of Impropriety

Once again, we look at where the behavior falls on the impropriety scale.

It's Okay
The message here is the same as it was in the action plan for Learned Behavior. Being able to show disappointment at the lack of results, rather than criticizing the other employee, will keep the lines of communication open. Allowing the other employee to feel your frustration through direct eye contact is an effective way to make your feelings known. Setting clear expectations for the future will allow you to keep the integrity of the relationship intact while sending a clear message that things must change.

It's Not Okay
Our concern once again is the cumulative effect of repeating a behavior that will eventually reach a tipping point. Demonstrating selfish tendencies, for instance, and a reluctance to share critical knowledge, can lead to alienation and a loss of respect. Issues of morality can be dangerous as well. While it could be argued that these are learned behaviors, the decision to execute them says a lot about a person's true character. The reality of the situation is that unethical practices call into question the employee's sense of morality. Regardless of any success that can be derived from these tactics, they can seriously affect the employee's credibility.

Our role in the Mentor Quadrant is to remind our employees of the character attributes that are common to people who have found extraordinary success. Despite the many material rewards that these successful people have earned, the thing they value most is their integrity, and the respect others have for them as a person. Employees who identify with the desire to emulate successful people will often adjust their behavior with that goal in mind.

It's Never Okay
Some of the most serious behavioral issues are emotionally driven. Because they tend to be far more intense, the damage that can be caused may be significant. Displaying rage towards another employee, holding a grudge, or sabotaging another employee's work because of jealous tendencies are all examples of some of the worst forms of inappropriate behavior.

The sense of urgency that is required to address situations that rise to this level is critical because the collateral damage that occurs is usually widespread. Sometimes the damage is so significant that it cannot be repaired, and the employee ends up marginalizing the role they will play in the company because of a lack of trust and respect from their peer group.

Step Two
Apologize Immediately

In this case, we are not looking for the source, because it is sitting right in front of us. The dialog that takes place in the Mentor Quadrant must begin with a full admission by the employee that the behavior was completely inappropriate and despite whatever triggered the altercation, no one else is to blame. The employee must be prepared to apologize directly to the affected parties, recognizing that there is a distinct possibility that their apology will not be accepted. They must show remorse and be prepared to accept whatever consequences result from their behavior, including the possibility of termination.

Step Three
Accept Full Accountability

Too often in these extreme cases, the employee looks for justification to defend their behavior. You must ensure that this is never permitted to happen. Under no circumstance will you allow them to place the blame anywhere other than where it belongs. It should be made clear that it will get them nowhere to argue that their behavior only happened because of the mistakes of others.

While your goal in the Mentor Quadrant is to provide counsel and to reassure your employee that despite the gravity of the situation, you have not lost faith in their ability to turn it around, they must be prepared to accept full responsibility for their conduct. While it's easy to criticize this type of behavior, it's important to understand that most of the people who possess these kinds of character flaws would dearly love to be rid of them. While the road ahead will be challenging, it is possible to overcome these hurdles with self-awareness and a strong desire to manage the behavior in the future.

Step Four
Walk the Talk

You need to be totally upfront with your employee and let them know that walking the talk may not be enough. It can be frustrating when the employee is making every effort to keep their behavior in check, but no one is buying it. It is the cold reality of the collateral damage that can be caused by these situations, and how difficult it can be to recover from a single outburst. Your job will be to continue to offer support and encouragement to your employee, and praise their effort to stay on the straight and narrow.

Remind them that eventually some people they have affected will recognize their effort and give them another chance. With new employees, they have a clean slate to work with, and it will be up to them to make the kinds of decisions that earn their respect. There may be little they can do to change the past, but the good news is that they have an opportunity to affect the future in a positive way.

Part Five

Lessons Learned Along the Way

Meetings versus Power Briefings	206
A Currency Called Experience	214
The Gift of Humility	218
And in The End	228

The difference between
the glass half full and the one half
empty is called momentum.

Meetings versus Power Briefings

Fall, 1992

Today marks the beginning of the budget process, and every department head is hard at work crunching numbers. Later this morning, I will meet with each of my five supervisors to review their preliminary sales and profit projections for the new year.

It's just after eight when I hear a familiar voice call my name. It's Ken Bathurst, head of human resources for Western Canada. Since my return to the company, Ken has been incredibly supportive. He's the only person besides Ron and Arnie, who knows anything about my condition. While I have been able to manage my worst episodes by discretely fading out of the public eye, I have sought Ken's council on many occasions, and his advice has proven invaluable.

His mission this morning is to inform every department head that there will be an important meeting in the main boardroom starting at noon. He asks that I take a good look at my calendar for the upcoming week and get ready to reschedule any commitments that are already in place. He inquires about the boys and suggests that next week I make arrangements to have my parents pick them up on Friday and keep them for the weekend since my return home will likely be delayed until late Sunday afternoon.

Return home from where? Where are we going? Before I have a chance to ask any questions, he is off. While our conversation has piqued my curiosity, I am quickly brought back to the task at hand as my first supervisor arrives to get things underway.

I am just finishing up with the second budget discussion as the noon hour approaches. As I make my way towards the boardroom, I suddenly remember that I have yet to do anything about next week's schedule. I decide to wait until I have a better idea of what is going on.

As I enter the room, I am met by two strangers who shake my hand and invite me to take a seat. As other department heads begin to file in, I take the opportunity to get a closer look at our visitors. Both men are tall and impeccably dressed. Their custom suits are of a high quality, cut to accentuate their broad shoulders and trim waistlines. Standing there, they remind me of a couple of sports commentators preparing to deliver their post-game analysis. Instead of formal introductions, the meeting begins with both men walking around the boardroom, presenting each of us with a small index card and requesting that we take a few moments to read it over carefully.

As I stare at the card, the first thing that catches my attention is the heading. It reads 'Indemnity Waiver' in bold print. There is dead silence for about thirty seconds until a lone voice cries out, "Gee Ken, I've heard of going to extreme lengths to fire a guy, but how can you call it a termination if the body is never found?"

The room erupts with laughter, but many of us are nervous. A quick review of the card suggests that the aforementioned company cannot be held liable for injuries resulting from physical activities that may include, but are not limited to, rappelling off a mountain cliff, traversing a steep ravine by zip-line, or long periods of exposure to inclement weather.

Before Ken makes his formal introductions, he attempts to lighten the mood by suggesting that there are several ways for a company to downsize in tough economic times, and this just happens to be one of the more creative ones

The two men who stand before us have impressive credentials and confirm my suspicion. They are former professional athletes who also happen to hold master's degrees in clinical and behavioral psychology. Their company works specifically with corporations, specializing in team synergy and relationship building in highly competitive environments. All of the workshops they conduct take place outdoors in remote areas. They call their program A Walk in the Woods. The sessions last one full week and everyone will be together twenty-four hours of every day.

We are asked to meet in the office parking lot next Monday morning at 5:30 a.m. From there we will be taken to an undisclosed location where there will be no phones or any other contact with anyone in the outside world unless a real emergency arises. We are told that we will be spending every waking hour outdoors, regardless of weather conditions. We will not be permitted to return to the home base until every daily task has been fully completed, no matter the hour. Each exercise is designed to test our ability to work effectively as a team, and to raise the stakes even higher; most tasks will involve some element of danger.

As the meeting draws to a close, we are handed a list of the things to bring with us. We are cautioned not to add anything to the list since all bags will be checked, and any unauthorized items will be confiscated.

When I was the head of the training department, I did a lot of research on corporate bonding exercises. The only conclusion I was able to draw from my reading was that the jury is still out as to how effective these experiences really are. In a company full of alpha personalities, this was going to be very interesting.

I am on my way back to my desk when Ken approaches and asks me to rejoin him in the boardroom. He tells me that he has a bit of a dilemma in that the conditions of the contract call for full disclosure of any medical conditions that could place a participant at risk. He asks me what I'd like to do about it, and I tell him that I'm not sure. As I leave, I promise to give him an answer before the day is out.

The whole thing makes me nervous, but after some serious self-reflection, I realize that my absence would not go unnoticed by my peer group. I know in my heart that despite the risk, this is going to be a once in a lifetime opportunity, so I opt to participate. The next day we meet with the two psychologists, and I do my best to give them a general overview of my symptoms, and what a typical episode is like for me. They assure me of total discretion and promise to remove me from the environment if I give them any indication that things are not right.

It turned out to be an incredible week with fond memories that have stayed with me ever since. I suffered no episodes and was able to partake in every challenge. The first exercise was one of the most memorable because it illustrated just how counter-productive highly competitive people can be when they fail to work together to find a solution. We were divided into two groups with no assigned leader or instructions other than to complete the task.

Our objective was to retrieve a raw egg from a tree stump that was partitioned by well-marked boundaries that we were not permitted to cross. The only materials at our disposal were a ball of string and a half dozen paper clips.

To say there was a serious lack of synergy would be an understatement. It was every man for himself, and each was determined to out-perform the other. In the end, neither team was able to recover the egg without breaking it.

When the exercise was over, we were gathered together for our first power debriefing. The objective was to have a free-flowing discussion of what went wrong, what we learned from the experience, and what we needed to do to prepare for our next challenge. Every member of the team was required to participate, without exception.

I should point out that these sessions always took place outdoors at the end of the day The bitter cold and howling winds were brutal. No matter how bad things got, we were never permitted to leave until every issue had been addressed to the satisfaction of our coaches. That meant that individuals were forced to confront one another, which usually led to other issues that were often far more personal in nature.

These were contentious sessions because of the competitive nature of the group, and the complex dynamic of each individual relationship. With the temperature rapidly dropping, we would huddle together like a herd of musk oxen, using each other's body heat to try to keep ourselves warm. Despite the bone chilling conditions, no session was ever cut short.

I remember one exchange in particular. It took place high up on the mountainside. We were perched on a cliff between two walls of solid granite. The winds were so loud, the only way you could be heard was to shout. This was one of our most challenging sessions that lasted well past dark. In the end, with flashlights in hand, we were able to successfully resolve some very tough issues.

Over the course of the week, we learned how to conduct a highly effective communication session by staying focused on what was really important, and by holding every person in attendance responsible for being part of the solution. By the time we were doing our last two power debriefings, everyone knew what would be expected of them, and we were able to tackle some tough issues and find real solutions in a fraction of the time it took to complete our earlier sessions.

When I returned home, I immediately took the concept and modified it for my business by turning traditional meetings into power briefings. The Walk in the Woods experience made me realize just how unproductive conventional meetings are. By the time I was ready to launch Quadrant Leadership, the only group communication vehicle I was interested in employing was a good power briefing.

Before I get into the elements that make up a highly effective power briefing, I would challenge anyone who is not ready to abandon traditional meetings to do yourself one simple favor. For your next meeting, complete a cost analysis to determine your return on investment. In the business world, we conduct so many meetings that we never seem to consider the cost implications. I promise that if you wasted as much money on other parts of your business as you do on meetings, you would quickly change your ways.

Start by calculating the real hard costs associated with the meeting, including the labor cost for everyone who attends, room fees if applicable, operating and office supplies, including audio-visual needs, and supplied food and beverages. Even if your only expense is the real cost of labor, you will find that most meetings will not pass the ROI test.

The real issue is that few meetings are results oriented. If they were, you would easily be able to calculate the actual sales that will be derived from the meeting or the costs savings that will result from a specific action taken during the meeting. The truth is that most meetings are simply communications sessions where the flow of information often travels in one direction. Once you conduct just one return on investment analysis, you will quickly see how costly meetings can be.

At minimum, you should debrief your meetings to determine if you are able to measure any return on investment at all. As an effective communication tool, most traditional meetings fair poorly. There is usually so much on the agenda that even as little as two hours later, many of the participants are hard pressed to tell you what the top three priorities were. A day later, most people remember less than fifty percent of what was covered.

When you consider what can be accomplished in a good power briefing, you may end up drawing the same conclusion that I did. Most meetings are simply a total waste of time and resources.

***

The nature of power briefings is that they are driven by need to know information. They are clear and concise, and action orientated. Power briefings incorporate a play on Pareto's law called the 20/80 rule. The objective is to try to articulate in twenty words what you used to say in eighty. With a little practice, the art of concise dialogue can easily be mastered.

Use bullet points and headlines to describe the topic and make sure the agenda is applicable to everyone who will attend the briefing. Everyone is required to participate. There is no room for complacency, and there are no principle speakers. The objective is to get to the point, determine what action or actions need to take place and then move on.

Power briefings do not require formal meeting rooms and can involve as little as one other person. You can conduct a power briefing almost anywhere, including on the run if necessary. Unlike traditional meetings, a power briefing can be repeated to suit the business and to work with employee schedules.

It is a highly effective communication vehicle for Quadrant Leadership. The idea that you are going to be spending so much time dedicated to employee development may make some of you wonder how on earth you are going to stay on top of everything else that is happening in your business. The answer is through power briefings. Once your managers or charge staff can deliver an effective power briefing, you will never again be concerned about being left in the dark.

Power briefings take a little practice before they become a natural occurrence. The biggest challenge is learning how to share important information in as few words as possible. The objective is not speed, although efficiency tends to be a side benefit. The primary objective of any power briefing is to get to the point, say what needs to be said, share whatever information is necessary, and then move on. If they sound a bit impersonal, that's because they are. You need to look at their purpose. The participants are not there for idle chatter. This is an action orientated fact driven communications session.

If I took away one simple thing from my incredible experience out there in the woods, it was that Pareto was right all along. Even when discussing important matters, eighty percent of our dialogue tends to contribute little to the solution. Once you can teach your people how to conduct an effective power briefing, the only traditional meeting you will endorse is one with a single theme that is action orientated and measurable.

Conducting an Effective Power Briefing

- The individual who calls the briefing should lead it.
- Every person in attendance is expected to participate.
- Use bullet points or headlines to open each point of discussion.
- Follow the 20/80 rule. When stating your case, keep your points short and concise.
- Power briefings are fact based, so stick only to the facts. Tell me what I need to know, not what you think I want to hear.
- If your comments are based on opinion, then make sure to state it that way.
- Keep the discussion on point. Do not allow anyone to change the subject. Stay in control of your power briefing.
- When looking for input, be specific about what your needs are. If there are deadlines involved, make sure that everyone is in agreement.
- End your power briefing with a concise recap, leaving no doubt as to what has been discussed and what has yet to be accomplished.

A Currency Called Experience

In the winter of 2009, I happened to be vacationing in Southern California. These were challenging times in the United States, following a significant downturn in the economy the year before. Official unemployment was hovering around the nine percent mark, but the real number was even worse. The one statistic that continues to go unreported is the percentage of workers who have simply given up and are no longer actively seeking employment. It is estimated that this group can add another two to three percent to the unemployment picture. The unfortunate reality of any economic downturn is that companies have no choice but to cut costs if they hope to survive. In doing so, many good people can get lost in the shuffle.

That winter, while staying at an RV resort in Desert Hot Springs, I met a man named Ryan Kirsch. His story made me realize that most companies are missing a huge opportunity.

At age forty-eight, Ryan lost his middle management job in a company that was not only downsizing, but also relocating its offices to the east coast. Unfortunately, for him and his wife Beth, her extreme arthritis meant that they had to remain in a dry climate. After being laid off, Ryan, a true optimist, started sending out hundreds of resumes. This was a man of many talents, including incredible people skills. He was a good listener, with a steady demeanor and a great sense of humor.

Beth shared with me that he received more that fifty cards and letters from co-workers and long time customers wishing him well. Ryan loved to work with tools, a jack-of-all-trades with no formal training. He was one of these guys who would take the time to work something through until he had a good idea of the mechanics. He would then proceed to fix it, demonstrating one of the most important attributes of an outstanding troubleshooter.

After their home had been foreclosed on, they decided to take the few funds that were left to purchase a class-A RV that would serve as their new residence. Once again, Ryan looked for the best solution to a tough situation with class and determination—critical attributes that good employers are constantly looking for.

When he was unable to find a job on his own, he turned to a headhunting agency that reviewed his resume and credentials, along with his work history. To his great surprise, they told him that his age was probably the reason he was not getting any responses. Apparently, at the ripe old age of forty-eight, Ryan was considered washed up. His frustration was easy to understand, so at the time I met him he had taken his resume off the market and was trying to figure things out.

After spending just a few days with this man I realized just how talented he was. There was no doubt in my mind that any boss who was smart enough to look past something as irrelevant as age would benefit enormously from this new acquisition to their business.

I wished him well but never forgot how dumbfounded I was that someone of his caliber could be so easily discarded. I guarantee that many of the companies he applied to are putting up with under-performers who could not hold a candle to his talent.

For many men and women like Ryan Kirsch, losing their livelihood can be devastating. Issues of self-esteem and self-worth can play havoc with physical health, and more often than not, place a heavy strain on personal relationships. I lost touch with Ryan but remained optimistic that someone would recognize his worth, and that he would soon be back on his feet.

Ryan's story should serve to remind every boss that when you discount an individual based solely on something as irrelevant as age, you do yourself a tremendous disservice.

When you take a moment to consider the value of real life experience, a reputation for reliability and accountability as well as good old fashion work ethic, then perhaps its time to reconsider this extraordinary resource.

Target your ads specifically to find these people. Use social media or other networking platforms to get your message out. They need to know that someone is looking for them and that someone values what they have to offer. It is important they hear that age is in no way an issue, because a smart boss knows that mutual respect knows no age boundaries. I can tell you that three good years of contribution from one extraordinary employee is worth of decade of mediocrity from another.

Here is another example to illustrate my point. About a year ago, I met a couple through a mutual friend at a party. Their names were Barry and Lou Ayers. Over the course of the evening, I had the opportunity to have a great conversation with Barry. I learned that he had been a manager with the Ingledew Shoe Company for an astonishing fifty years.

Ingledew's is a Canadian owned and operated company with a well-established brand that specializes in high-quality apparel. When it came time to do research for this book, I asked Barry if he would sit down with me and chat about his personal experience. Our conversation touched on many subjects, from his definition of extraordinary customer service to the role hands-on management can play in a company's success. I realized while conducting the interview what an amazing resource people like Barry could be for any boss looking for insight and inspiration on how to get things right.

Barry's company worked on a commission basis, so his bread and butter depended on repeat business. When asked about the role outstanding customer service played in his success, he talked about what it took to build not only the company's reputation but his reputation as well. He discussed the importance of loyalty and of protecting the brand by knowing everything about it. As Barry would say, no customer should know more about what you are selling than you do. While listening to his words, I knew that I was in the presence of someone who had walked the talk.

I could not help but think how valuable his feedback could be for new employees just starting out. His stories alone would command their respect. One example he gave me was when he was working at a location in the business district. His clients were men and women who had a high regard for fashion and clearly understood the role it played in their personal success. These were busy people who were constantly on the go. At their request, Barry would arrive at the store two hours before opening, just to make sure they got the personal service they had come to expect from him. No one told Barry to do this; it may even have been against store policy, but Barry understood what it meant to go above and beyond to demonstrate to his customers just how much he valued their business. Clearly, it paid off for him. His enduring career speaks for itself.

Even though Barry has been retired for several years now, he confessed that he cannot help looking for ways to make things better. It just goes to prove that these kinds of philosophies are firmly entrenched in those who have a well-deserved reputation for delivering the difference on a daily basis. There is no doubt in my mind that if Barry Ayers were asked to come back and put on a service clinic for any company who offered the invitation, he would be there in a heartbeat. One thing I know for sure is that his insight would be well worth everyone's time.

As a member of a younger generation of bosses, you must never take for granted the people who show you a genuine appreciation for the opportunity to grow and develop in your company. There is no question in my mind that by reaching out to the network of displaced workers who have simply stopped looking for employment, you are tapping into pure gold. Age discrimination is perhaps the most unfortunate consequence of a society that today seems obsessed with youth. Perhaps the lesson here is a simple one: Like a good fine wine, you may discover that your best employees are those who get better with age.

The Gift of Humility

Ronald McDonald House

December 25, 1994

Christmas morning and the house is still, the sound of youthful exuberance and excited anticipation no longer present. It is hard to believe that it has been four years since my divorce. While I have come to enjoy my life as a single dad, this is the one day of the year when my heart longs for days gone by.

I will not see the boys today; a decision I have come to accept. For the children of broken homes and shared custody, this is often a day of travel. Handed off from one loving parent to the next, the clock ticking, these are the true peacekeepers in this season of good will.

I recall my own childhood and how my parents would never travel on Christmas Day, no matter who offered the invitation. As far as they were concerned, Christmas Day was for the children to play and enjoy their treasures. Their selfless act is the reason I make no claim on this day. I take satisfaction in knowing that tomorrow will be our day.

As I stare out the window, I am drawn to the sullen sky. While I have never subscribed to the notion that my episodes can be triggered by weather, I cannot deny that I fare much better in sunshine.

For me, most of my days are like strolling down the deck of a giant ocean liner. When the seas are calm, the effort is free and easy, but as the waves begin to crest, and the great boat is tossed from side to side, balance becomes my top priority. So much of my life is about finding my internal balance. On those occasions when I am unable to take refuge from the most treacherous of storms, I hold on tight and pray that I will not be swept overboard.

On the one day of the year when I feel the greatest sense of loss, I am overcome with feelings of enormous self-pity. Life just doesn't seem to be fair. I am so tired of the roller coaster of emotions that continue to push my mental and physical welfare to the brink. I can barely remember what normal feels like.

The great irony is that I have so much to celebrate. My first year in business has been a resounding success, and save for a few minor setbacks in the beginning; I am on solid ground. We are making excellent progress with Quadrant Leadership, and my company's results have far exceeded my expectations. In every sense of the word, I should be jumping for joy, and yet I choose to dwell on my misfortunes.

As the alarm clock suddenly springs to life, I groan. While I would like nothing more than to pull the covers over my head and sleep the entire day away, I remember the promise I made to Anne. Regardless of how I might feel, I will not let her down.

***

November 6, 1994

Today I am attending an owner/operator's meeting at our regional office in Burnaby. This is the same facility where I spent many years on the corporate side of McDonald's, working in both the operations and training departments.

I am about to make my way into the meeting room when I see my former secretary, Linda. She is waving in my direction. After a minute playing catch-up, she tells me that she just got a call from Ronald McDonald House. For anyone unfamiliar with Ronald House, it's a not-for-profit organization that provides accommodations for sick children with life-threatening illnesses and their immediate family members. The only stipulation is that the family must live outside of the major metropolitan areas, making travel their only option to receive treatment.

The original Vancouver Ronald House is located on Angus Drive in the upscale neighborhood of Shaughnessy on the west side of the city. It is a beautiful old manor that in 1983 was converted to a thirteen bedroom facility. It is close to Vancouver Children's Hospital, making it an ideal location.

Linda tells me that Anne, the house manager, is looking for volunteers to help out on Christmas Day. Since my restaurant is close by, she thought there might be someone on my staff who would be interested in helping out. I let her know that I will start making inquiries as soon as I get back to the restaurant.

In 1994, the Vancouver Ronald McDonald House was one of only a handful of Ronald Houses in all of North America that remained open on Christmas Day. In most cities, families staying at the house are required to make temporary relocation arrangements.

Anne is a remarkable woman. She has made it clear that her goal is to keep the house open on Christmas Day. She knows how difficult and expensive it can be for families to find temporary accommodation in a city like Vancouver. She is also aware of how any disruption to a sick child's routine can affect their health and welfare. Even though she will be traveling back to England to be with her own family for the holidays, she is determined to make this happen.

A few days later, I call her up. While we have never formerly met, our paths have crossed at many fundraisers. This will mark the first time we will speak one on one. I let her know that I have a few promising leads, but so far no firm commitments. I take the opportunity to get a better idea of what the job entails, and the time commitment that will be involved. Anne explains that the biggest job will be to prepare a traditional Christmas dinner for all the families staying at the house, as well as any relatives who will be joining them. This year the number is expected to be between forty-five and fifty people.

She goes on to explain that while every bit of help is appreciated, what she's really looking for is someone who is prepared to spend the entire day at the house, preparing the meal, setting up all of the tables for dinner, and then remaining behind to do the massive cleanup. As I listen to the heady job description, I quickly realize that none of my employees will be able to make such a major commitment on Christmas Day. I am about to tell her when it suddenly dawns on me that I do know someone who will not only be free for the entire day but is more than capable of doing the job.

She is delighted with the news, thanks me for my generous commitment, and tells me that I have taken a huge weight off her shoulders.

***

Christmas Day

It is just past ten a.m. when I arrive at the house. As I ascend the staircase, I see that most of the lights on the main floor are off. I am unsure whether I should simply walk in or wait for an invitation. I decide that since no one knows who I am, I will ring the doorbell.

It's one of those old fashion knobs shaped like the end of a key. You must turn it all the way around to generate a sound.

After three unsuccessful attempts to capture anyone's attention, I am about to try the doorknob when I hear the pitter-patter of tiny feet running across a hard surface. Seconds later, the door swings open and I am greeted by a little boy no more than five years old. The tiny wisps of hair atop his head are climaxed only by his enormous chubby red cheeks. He is dressed in blue jeans and a Superman T-shirt that does little to cover his distended stomach, leaving his outie belly button to fend for itself. Before I can ask him if there are any adults I might talk to, he is off.

As I step into the dimly lit foyer, I can see an office to my immediate left and a sitting room to my right. Farther down the hall, I see light streaming from the kitchen. As I approach, I hear voices.

"I just saw a car pull up. I think it might be the McDonald's guy Anne was talking about."

"Do you think he'll have the answer?"

"He should, he's in the restaurant business."

Personal experience has taught me that it's never a good idea to eavesdrop on someone else's conversation, even when it appears that you are the subject of discussion. I wait just long enough for the room to grow silent before rounding the corner.

With initial introductions out of the way, I am relieved to find out that both ladies are regular volunteers. Their only concern is that neither has cooked at the house before, let alone for fifty people. They draw my attention to the objects of their previous conversation. There, sitting atop the industrial ovens, are two of the biggest turkeys I have ever seen in my life. Each bird weighs more than 37 pounds. They tell me that so far they have not been able to find a cookbook with instructions for a turkey of this size. Without the Internet to search or a YouTube video to watch on the secrets to cooking a behemoth turkey, we are on our own.

I can see that the ladies are looking to me for direction. As they wait for me to speak, I realize just how important it is that we get this right. I recommended that they each call their family and friends to see if anyone can provide them with some useful information. While they are busy doing that, my job will be to pull all the ingredients together to prepare the stuffing. So far I have not seen another soul, save for my little friend, so we will not bother anyone staying at the house.

As I begin my quest, I am struck by the sheer size of the kitchen. It is enormous and extremely well designed, with plenty of room for each family to have its own utensil drawers and cupboard space. Germs are a real concern in an environment like this, so sharing is out of the question. All the appliances are of industrial quality, and the dishwashers are set to extremely high temperatures for optimum sanitation. The center Island is massive, lined with row upon row of pullout drawers full of pots and pans of every size. It takes me several minutes to gather all my ingredients. By the time I am ready to start, the ladies have returned from their calls. With input from three reliable sources, the consensus is that we will make sure the turkeys are in the oven by no later than 11:30 a.m. With the first big decision of the morning out of the way, we're off and running.

I am busy scoring a huge pot of Brussels sprouts when the little boy reappears. This time, he has his mother in tow. As they enter the kitchen, I introduce myself. I tell her that her son would make an excellent doorman. She points him in the direction of the tables located at the far end of the kitchen.

Just as I am transferring my pot of sprouts to the top of the stove, I hear her say, "Are you ready, little man?" When I look up, I can see that she has just finished preparing a syringe filled with clear liquid. As he turns his head, she pierces his flesh in one quick motion and begins to press down on the plunger. He flinches but does not cry out. Instead, he holds his breath until she removes the needle. She places a small piece of cotton batten on the puncture wound and without a word of instruction he takes hold of it and applies pressure with his tiny little fingers.

"Can I have a Spiderman Band-Aid, Mommy?"

"Of course you can sweetie. Just remember that there are only three of those left.

With the Band-Aid firmly affixed, he heads off on another adventure.

I shake my head as I speak. "That was amazing. How old is he?"

"He turns five in three weeks. I am learning how to do all his injections so that we can go home. He spent nearly two months in Children's Hospital, and we have been here at Ronald House for a little over a month. I have two other children at home I have not seen in several weeks. I talk to them every day on the phone, but they are having a very tough time."

"Did they not come down for the Christmas holidays?"

"No, they are still back home in Creston. It's just so expensive, and when we brought Tyler down to the hospital, my husband had to use up all his holidays. I've got my fingers crossed that the doctor will give us the okay to go home next week.

As she draws near, I can see the dark circles of restless sleep. Clearly, the demands of caring for a sick child have taken a great toll on her.

"Is there anything I can do to help?" she asks.

"I think we are good, but thanks for offering. Why don't you just enjoy your Christmas day?"

As soon as it is out of my mouth, I realize how ridiculous that must sound to her. She gives me a tired smile and says, "Believe me when I say that I wish I could.

As I watch her ascend the stairs, I feel like such a fool. I have been so consumed by self-pity that I did not even stop to consider what the people in this house are going through. I doubt any of them were looking forward to spending Christmas day at Ronald House. I have been brooding over something as trivial as not being able to see my boys today. I have just met a woman who has not seen her daughters in weeks, and her precious little boy is fighting for his life.

I am so ashamed of my behavior that I begin to feel nauseous. How could I have been so incredibly self-absorbed? It is embarrassing to think that my plight was so much worse than anyone else's.

Parents in this house are faced with the very real possibility that their child might die. As a Dad, I cannot begin to imagine their pain.

As I struggle to regain my composure, I suddenly remember something my old friend Brian Midgley once told me. I had confessed to him that I had handled a tough situation badly and wanted his advice on how to make it right. He said that if I truly regretted my actions, I must begin by forgiving myself. It is only by forgiving ourselves that we can reset the compass in our mind that will clear the path to a better decision. I never forgot his words and realize I must start right now. Through forgiveness, I am able to rid myself of the guilt that has made me feel like such a fool.

I am now convinced that my coming here today was in no way a coincidence. This whole experience was meant to be. I have been properly humbled and for that, I am truly grateful. The invisible chains that have tied me to my illness from the beginning have been torn free. Never again will I allow myself an ounce of self-pity. I may not like what I have to deal with, but I will not let my illness make me a victim.

I feel a genuine sense of joy, and like a breath of fresh air, I am completely energized and ready to take on the rest of the day.

As the noon hour draws near, more families begin to appear. Anne requested that we take our break over the lunch hour to allow each family their personal space in the kitchen. I am just sitting down to a nice cup of tea when a little girl of about ten approaches. She is wearing a baseball cap that reads, "Hair is highly overrated."

"Are you the man who owns McDonald's?" she asks.

"Well I don't own all of them, but I do own one."

Here eyes widen as the rumor is confirmed.

"Do you like McDonald's?" I smile.

"Oh yes. I love Chicken McNuggets with lots of ketchup. My mom says when I get better we can go to McDonald's, and I can have a Happy Meal."

Just then, I notice that she is wearing a Disney T-shirt with the 101 Dalmatians theme.

"I like your T-shirt. Did you know that McDonald's was giving out the Dalmatians in Happy Meals just a few months ago?"

She nods her head yes and tells me that 101 Dalmatians is her favorite Disney movie. She then tells me that she only got a chance to collect four Dalmatians before she got sick.

I tell her that's too bad, and then add, "How would you like to have them all?"

She looks at me in disbelief.

"I'll tell you what. You go get your mom so we can make sure it's all right with her. If she says it's okay, I'll have someone bring over all 101 tomorrow."

Without the slightest warning, she lets out one of those ear-piercing screams that only a ten-year-old girl is capable of. Before I have a chance to tell her I will also include some Chicken McNuggets for her and any of the other kids in the house that would like some, she's off to find her mother. Her quick departure may have just saved my eardrums from a second assault.

The dinner goes off without a hitch. Both turkeys were done to perfection, and we got many positive comments on how moist and tender it was. I am completely exhausted when I leave the house at nine p.m. I will sleep well tonight. Tomorrow, I'll pick up the boys, and we'll spend the entire day together.

It has become a tradition that the group of weekend warriors that make up my "family of men" will also be joining us. I look forward to seeing them all, and there will be presents under the tree for everyone.

I will likely hug the boys a little tighter and for a little longer than they would prefer, but I will do it just the same.

***

That Christmas would mark the first of ten consecutive Christmas days that I would spend at Ronald House.[2] Each as special as the last, and each, a gentle reminder that no matter how tough I think I might have it, there will always be someone, somewhere, who is dealing with something far worse than I. When I return to work after the holidays, I allow myself the opportunity to enjoy the fruits of my labor. I have managed to make Quadrant Leadership an intricate part of my business, and now as a new year dawns, I look forward to seeing just how much more we can accomplish.

I highly recommend that every boss take the time to volunteer their services somewhere where they are not always the person in charge. Playing the best supporting role you possibly can, will serve to remind you just how important every job in your own business is. Leadership is not always about being the final decision maker. Sometimes it's about letting other people play that role. It takes nothing away from who you are. If anything, it shows great wisdom.

One of the most common misnomers about Quadrant Leadership is that you are giving up many of the things that leaders are supposed to do. I would argue that the role of a leader is to achieve the best results in the most ethical way possible. How you go about accomplishing that task has nothing to do with the paradigm of leadership to which so many people subscribe. Your most important job is to build a successful business. In the end, if you are able to provide others with the kind of insight and knowledge that will serve them well as they continue their journey in life, then how can that be anything but good?

---

[2] One of the biggest misconceptions about Ronald McDonald House is that it is fully funded by McDonald's Restaurants. While the corporation and affiliated owner/operators actively support all of the houses in North America through a variety of fundraising endeavors, each Ronald House is a stand-alone, non-profit organization that must continually raise funds to meet its annual operating budget. I invite you to give generously to the house that love built.

And in The End

THE BEAST

Sunlight does wonders for my illness, so every winter I make it a priority to spend as much time as possible in Southern California. I have a small camper van that serves as my mobile home away from home. I call her The Beast and even though she is now more than thirty years old, she is in remarkable shape and incredibly reliable. My destination for this trip is a beautiful park just north of the Mexican border. It is located in the historic town of Chula Vista and sits adjacent to the local marina. I am looking forward to getting settled in. I have reserved a premium spot complete with spectacular ocean views. So far, the trip down has been uneventful. I have made excellent time this morning, and since my day began well before sunrise, I am looking forward to a nice leisurely breakfast.

Five minutes later, I am exiting the freeway. The off-ramp rises slightly before turning sharply to the right. As I approach my first intersection, I spot a small directional sign. Weathered by a steady diet of sun and wind, the letters are badly faded and impossible to read. Fortunately for me, the terrain is flat and unobstructed. A quick scan of the horizon reveals the outline of several buildings to the west. As I draw closer, I am surprised to discover that what resembled a small town from a distance is, in fact, a large industrial park. The warehouses and loading bays that occupy the park are situated on beautifully tree-lined streets that betray the primary purpose for the facility. I am so preoccupied with my surroundings that I quickly lose all sense of direction. Before I am drawn too far into the maze, I pull over to assess my situation.

Without the benefit of a GPS system to guide my way, I resign myself to the fact that good old-fashioned trial and error will be my only recourse. The persistent drone of the freeway tells me that the exit is close. Now all I have to do is find it. I am so caught up in contemplating my next move that I fail to see the stranger approach. The sound of the young man's voice breaks my concentration, and I react by jumping clear off my seat.

"Are you lost?"

As I struggle to regain my composure, I say, "My God, you scared me half to death."

"Sorry about that, man, you just looked like you could use a little help."

As he speaks, I get my first opportunity to assess the young man standing before me. Although I suspect his age to be no more than thirty, the prominent lines that run deep across his weathered face are reminiscent of a life hard-lived. He is tall and thin. His clothes hang loose upon his narrow frame.

Despite his outward appearance, there is an easy look to him. His eyes reveal a kindness that immediately puts me at ease.

"I guess I could use your help after all. Thank you. I just came off the freeway and was looking for a gas station and a bite to eat when somehow I managed to get myself into this mess."

He shakes his head before saying, "The road you are looking for is poorly marked. It is easy to see how you got confused. It's a good thing that this is a weekend. The rest of the week, this place is filled with hundreds of trucks and trailers. Do you have a pen and a piece of paper handy? I will be happy to get you back on your way."

Retrieving my computer bag, I turn to a blank page in my notebook and begin to write. When I am done, I repeat the directions back to him, and he nods.

"You will pass right by a gas station and a number of restaurants on your way to the freeway ramp. You can't miss it."

I thank him and begin to pull a few dollar bills out of my pocket.

He puts his hand up to indicate that I should stop. "You can keep your money; I really don't have much use for it.

Before I can comment, he points to my passenger seat. "If it's all right with you, I'll take that banana off your hands."

Without hesitation, I say, "My pleasure, but why not take the cash as well?"

He pauses before he answers. "The truth is, man, I'm not exactly popular with the local merchants around here. I'd likely be thrown out before I could even prove that I could pay. You see, sometimes I get so hungry that I am forced to steal to feed myself. I'm not proud of it, but I get desperate. If I show my face anywhere near one of those stores in broad daylight, they'll call the cops on me for sure."

I feel for him, but I can think of nothing else that will help his situation. I thank him again and start my engine.

True to his word, his directions are spot-on, and a number of restaurants begin to come into view. An hour later, I am filling my gas tank when I recognize a familiar image reflecting off my tinted window. A few minutes later, I am ordering at the drive-thru speaker. Reversing my directions, I find him leaning under a shade tree.

"Don't tell me you're still lost," he says.

"No, not at all. I came back to give you something."

As he stares in disbelief, I hand him two bags. The first contains a quarter pounder meal, super-sized with two apple pies and a half dozen boxes of McDonald's cookies. The other bag contains an assortment of fresh fruits from the convenience store located next to the gas station. The look on his face tells me all I need to know.

As he slowly examines the contents of both bags, I take the opportunity to say simply, "You're a good man, and you should never forget that. I wish you well, and I thank you again."

He stares at my van as it slowly disappears down the road. A few minutes later, I am back on the freeway. I drive in silence, content in knowing that I have done the right thing. Life is full of choices. I learned a long time ago that if something feels right and is worth doing, then it's always worth the effort.

For me, Quadrant Leadership was worth every bit of effort I put into it. When I first set out to find a way to keep my company operating when I knew that I could not, I had no idea that it would evolve into something so remarkable. My only regret is not sharing it sooner. If you asked me if I would ever return to a traditional way of leading a group of people, my answer would be a resounding no. There is no doubt in my mind that the pure satisfaction derived from Quadrant Leadership would make it a simple choice for me.

The model does not specifically address succession planning, but I think it is safe to say that you will never run short of future leaders eager for an opportunity to run your company. Their leadership style cannot help but reflect yours. After all, their whole development has been about acquiring knowledge in order to lead the way. I can't think of a more qualified candidate than that.

***

The year 2001 was difficult for me. I gained over seventy pounds and was beginning to spend long periods away from my business. In my mind, I was losing the battle. It was time to make my health my number one priority. That fall I made things official by placing my company up for sale. It was an extremely difficult decision to make, but in my heart, I knew it was the right thing to do. Two extraordinary things happened that year that speak to the power of Quadrant Leadership and its incredible sustainability. As I have just stated, I was now missing a great deal of work and my personal contribution to my own company was the least it had ever been.

It was during this time that the McDonald's corporation decided to introduce a silent shopper program to rate all of the restaurants from a customer's perspective. McDonald's has always done internal critiques, but this marked the first time that we would be assessed based solely on customer feedback. Every operator across Western Canada would have their restaurants visited several times by these secret shoppers. They would measure the same QSC that Ray Kroc believed was the most important part of the McDonald's success story. Outstanding restaurant operations would be the criteria.

When the program ended, and the results were tallied, two of my restaurants scored in the top ten of the more than three hundred operator restaurants that participated in the program. One of my restaurants was in the top three. To have one location in the top ten would have been an outstanding achievement, but to have two was truly remarkable. Clearly, the strength of the Quadrant Leadership Model carried the day. I was so proud of my people. Even when I could not be there for them, they were there for me in a big way.

The other amazing achievement relates specifically to my employees themselves. It's traditional that operators give out one scholarship each year to a deserving employee who will be continuing their education. In 2001, I decided that I would not put a limit on the number of scholarships that could be awarded. I made it known that any graduate was eligible to earn a scholarship. The criteria to qualify were set very high. They involved a combination of maintaining excellent grades while making a significant contribution to the company. I set aside funding for five scholarships at the beginning of the school year.

When it came time to assess who had qualified, the numbers were truly impressive. Come ceremony time, I would be awarding an unprecedented eleven scholarships. At one of the two local high schools that my employees attended, I was given my own section of the awards program to recognize eight remarkable students. Each of the winners was more than deserving, and every one of them had clearly shown what they were truly capable of.

On July 18, 2002, I said goodbye to my people and my company for the last time. In my heart, I knew I would never return. In 1997, I relocated to the Comox Valley on Vancouver Island. In a small town, you forge some close business relationships, and I had a good one with the local radio station. They were kind enough to invite me on air so that I could thank my many customers, and, of course, my wonderful staff for their incredible contribution to my company over the years. It was a fitting conclusion to a thirty-two-year journey.

***

Being bipolar is a reality in my life, and unlike some people who are fortunate enough to have periods of remission, mine is a constant companion. There is no doubt that I will continue to have good and bad days, but I know for certain that I will never let it define who I am as a person. This book marks the first time I have ever written the words bipolar disorder. I have stood steadfast in my belief that I will not give it voice, or even acknowledge its existence. It is my way of taking away any power it might have over me. I have never used it as an excuse, and I never will.

There is a photo that sits on my window sill. It is a picture taken of my sons when they were little boys atop Whistler Mountain. My oldest son has his arm wrapped around his younger brother, a symbol of the extraordinary bond that exists between these two incredible young men, even to this day. Over the years, whenever I found myself faced with the worst that my disease could throw at me, I would hold that picture close to my chest. It would remind me that I have so much to be grateful for, and it would give me the courage and the strength to carry on.

These days there is another picture that shares a place of honor on the same window sill. It is of two adorable little girls who just happen to be my beautiful granddaughters. These precious little angels are my new inspiration. When I think of them, it makes me smile. Simply knowing they breathe and walk this earth lifts me high above the darkest clouds, and once again, I walk in sunlight.

I would like to thank a very special group of
people who have enriched my life in the best
possible way. I owe them more than they will ever know.

Terry Vato
Lori Liptrot
Tina Harrower
Robert Thorley
Bernie Lee McDougall
Evelyn and Rick Dolley
Di and Tony Robertson
Carol and John Uszkalo
Josie and Jerry Miachika
Brenda and Darryl McDougall

Printed in Canada